Good Housekeeping

Stain
RESCUE!

Good Housekeeping

Stain

RESCUE!

THE A-Z GUIDE TO REMOVING SMUDGES, SPOTS & SPILLS

WITHDRAWN

HEARST BOOKS
New York

Contents

Introduction

Life can be messy—literally! Whether you're throwing a party, playing in your backyard, painting your bedroom, working on your car, or simply enjoying a family dinner at home, chances are that you'll end up with a stain. And it doesn't matter if that stain is on your clothes, your upholstery, or your carpet: You need to know how to get it out.

This guide provides immediate, easy-to-follow answers to all your stain questions. Not sure how to get out the catsup that ended up on your shirt after your annual family picnic? What about the grease that got tracked onto your carpet? Or the crayon that mysteriously now decorates your living room couch? You'll discover how to remove these and hundreds of other stains quickly and easily from fabrics, carpet, and upholstery in the book's handy "A-to-Z Stain-Removal Guide" (Chapter 3).

You'll also discover surprising and important information on the best ways to use bleach, which stain-removal tools and products you should have on hand, how to identify mystery stains, the best ways to prevent stains, how to treat and store heirloom textiles, and much more. You can even find how to remove the top ten kid stains!

(If you are unsure about the cleaning requirements for your fabric, carpet, or upholstery, be sure to test your stain-removal method on a hidden spot. If you see any evidence of damage—such as loss of color or a change in texture—or if you are unsure about the method's safety for your fabric, consult a professional dry cleaner or a professional upholstery or carpet cleaner for advice.)

All this invaluable stain-removal advice comes straight from the cleaning experts at the Good Housekeeping Research Institute. For more than 100 years, the Good Housekeeping Research Institute has evaluated household products, offered helpful advice, and championed the rights of consumers. It is also the driving force behind the Good Housekeeping Seal, the trusted icon awarded to products that are backed by a limited warranty from the Good Housekeeping Research Institute.

With this book at your side, you have all the help you need to remove even the trickiest stains. Use it whenever life—or a messy toddler—tosses a stain your way.

—*The Good Housekeeping Research Institute*

one

Laundry Lowdown

W hy, you ask, would a book about stain removal begin with a chapter on laundry techniques? The answer is simple: Doing your laundry the wrong way can permanently set existing stains . . . and even create a few new ones. Doing it the right way means that many stains will disappear with minimal effort.

The Laundry Basics

Having the right products on hand makes everything easier!

DETERGENT

Because they perform better in both hard and soft water, detergents have essentially replaced old-fashioned laundry soap for laundering. They are available in liquid or granule forms, with or without additives such as oxygen bleach and fabric softener, and in formulas designed for specific uses, such as cold-water wash or high efficiency for low-sudsing front- or top-loading water-saving washing machines.

PREWASH STAIN & SOIL REMOVERS

Pretreatment products are available in many forms: aerosols, pump sprays, sticks, foams, gels, and liquids. Choose the most convenient one for you and use it as recommended for your kind of fabric and type of stain. These products are solvent-based—which means petroleum-based or detergent-based—so they work especially well on removing oil-based stains from man-made fibers such as polyester.

BLEACH

There are two types: chlorine and nonchlorine (or oxygen) bleach. The garment's care label will tell you which one is safe for your particular item or if you should avoid bleach altogether. Some trims, buttons, and elastics may not react well to bleach. So while bleach might be safe for the fabric, it may not be safe for the whole item. Follow care instructions for best results.

Chlorine Bleach

Helps remove stains but can also strip away the color and/or damage certain fibers. It also acts as a disinfectant on bacteria and viruses, which is why it is so useful for items like cloth diapers and baby bibs. Chlorine bleach works faster and is more effective in restoring whiteness than oxygen bleach, but it can weaken fibers if not used correctly. Chlorine bleach is not safe for silk, wool, mohair, leather, or spandex.

Nonchlorine or Oxygen Bleach

Helps clean and brighten dingy items. Although it is often called "all-fabric bleach," it may damage silk, wool, acetate, and some flame-retardant fabrics. Check the care label. Note that some detergents have oxygen bleach as an additive.

FABRIC SOFTENER

This product makes clothes and household items feel soft and fluffy; it also decreases static cling. In addition, permanent-press fabrics treated with softener tend to dry faster and wrinkle less. However, it reduces the effectiveness of flame-retardant finishes on children's sleepwear and can inhibit the moisture-management characteristics of high-performance fabrics used in active sportswear. Towels treated with too much fabric softener become less absorbent. In liquid form, fabric softener is added to the wash during the final stages of the rinse cycle. It is also available as packets or sheets that go into the dryer or as an additive in some laundry detergents. Whether you use fabric softener is a matter of personal preference.

Sort Smart

So you've dragged those soiled and dirty clothes over to the washing machine. Now what? The first step is to sort them into appropriate wash loads. Eventually, all laundry has to be sorted by:

1 Color (whites and/or lights, darks)
2 Recommended water temperature (cold, warm, or hot)
3 Type of wash cycle (regular or cottons, permanent press or casual, delicate, hand wash)
4 Type of bleach that is safe to use on the fabric (chlorine or nonchlorine/oxygen)

How you begin to sort will depend on the type of items you have. The first sort—by color—is easy because all you have to do is look at the items. Further sorting means you have to consult the care labels to determine the recommended wash cycle, water temperature, and bleach recommendations. Some care labels include printed instructions; others use symbols. Check out "Your Guide to Fabric Care Symbols" on page 23 to find out what these symbols mean.

Sort 1: By Color

Put all the darks in one pile, all the lights in another. As you sort by color, check for spots and stains. Check the pockets, too. If candy, crayons, or pens are left in the pockets, they will stain clothes during washing. As you sort, pretreat stains. Check out Chapter 2, "First Aid for Stains," for more information. If you know the source of the stain, consult Chapter 3, "The A-to-Z Stain-Removal Guide," before pretreating it.

• *Color alert!* It's not always easy to decide if an item belongs in the "dark" or "light" pile. Often, it's a judgment call: prints with a dark background or predominantly dark colors go in the "dark" pile; prints with a light background or predominantly light colors go in the "light" pile. If you are dealing with a two-tone item, such as a dress with a white bodice and a black skirt, launder it separately the first few times, following the care-label instructions. If the dark colors run or fade, return the item to the store for a refund.

• *Red alert!* Brightly colored fabrics (especially red) and dark or overdyed items (especially jeans) may shed some of their color when first washed. To avoid transferring the dye to other items, launder new items separately the first few times. To be sure the

WATER TEMPERATURE & STAIN REMOVAL

Although hot water is sometimes the best choice for laundry, it's not recommended for general stain removal. With hot water, you run the risk of setting the stain rather than removing it. Instead, depending on the type of stain and its location (fabric, upholstery, or carpet), either cool or cold water is recommended.

Cool water (85°–100°F or 29°–38°C) is gentle on fabrics and minimizes chances of dye loss.

Cold water (65°–85°F or 18°–29°C) is particularly effective on certain types of stains, such as blood. It is also recommended as the final rinse on upholstery and carpet because it will remove any previously used solutions without harming sensitive dyes.

color has stopped running, add an old white sock or handkerchief to the wash. If it comes out as white as it went in, you can safely wash the bright items with the rest of your laundry.

- *Fuzz alert!* Items that may shed fuzzies should be washed separately. These include towels and anything made from chenille fabric. Sweatshirts and flannel items can also shed the first few times they are washed. Toss them in the wash with like-colored towels for the first few launderings.

Sort 2: By Water Temperature

Once upon a time, people believed that the only way to get clothes clean was to use the hottest water possible. But with the advent of improved laundry products, this is no longer true.

The garment's care label has recommendations for water temperature. One reason to follow these recommendations is to avoid shrinkage. But there are other reasons:

- Water that is too hot can cause colors to fade, making garments look old and tired before their time.

- Lower water temperatures minimize wrinkling.

HOT WATER (110°–140°F or 43°–63°C) is the best choice for most heavily soiled items or items that must be as clean as possible, such as diapers. However, temperatures this high may cause unstable dyes to run or fade, can cause wrinkling in permanent-press fabrics, and may cause items to shrink.

WARM WATER (100°–110° F or 38°–43°C) minimizes the chance of shrinkage and is gentler on the fabrics, resulting in fewer wrinkles and less chance of dye loss.

Washing items in a higher-than-recommended water temperature is risky business; using a lower temperature is always a safe bet.

COLD WATER (65°–85°F or 18°–29°C) helps protect sensitive dyes and further minimizes any chance of shrinkage. It's the least effective temperature range for very dirty clothes but is a fine choice for lightly soiled loads.

Sort 3: By Wash Cycle Setting

REGULAR (heavy duty or cottons) setting has the most agitation, so it should be reserved for sturdy or heavily soiled clothes.

PERMANENT PRESS (casual or colored) setting has a shorter agitation time and an extra cold-water spray or deep rinse that minimizes wrinkles. Use this setting for synthetics and clothes that have a moderate amount of soil.

GENTLE or DELICATE KNITS setting has slower and shorter or intermittent agitation and spin cycles. It's generally recommended for lingerie, sheer or rayon fabrics, and machine-washable silks and wools.

ENERGY SAVER

If your hot-water supply is limited, start with the hot-water wash loads, then follow with warm, then cold.

Sort 4: By Bleach Requirements

As a general rule, you can eliminate the "dark fabrics" pile from this sorting step. In all likelihood, you won't need to bleach the darks unless you have a spot or stain that requires special treatment with oxygen (nonchlorine) bleach. (See Chapter 3, "The A-to-Z Stain-Removal Guide.")

Check the care labels to find out if bleach is safe for the item and which type of bleach you should use.

Wash Right

Now it's time to put those items into the washing machine. Believe it or not, there's a right way to do this, too. No matter which type of laundry detergent you choose, check the package for the right amount to use. Using too little detergent may not get your clothes clean. Using too much doesn't mean cleaner clothes; it just means you are wasting your money.

Set the washing machine to its smallest load level and fill with water. Then add the recommended amount of detergent and let the machine agitate long enough to dissolve the detergent and make some suds. If you are adding bleach and want to do it most efficiently, add it next, directly into the water and let the machine agitate for about 30 seconds, or use the machine's bleach dispenser. NOW add the clothes, reset the machine for the desired size load, and let it do its work.

If clothes are heavily soiled, once the washer is filled to the desired water level, turn the machine off and let everything soak for about 30 minutes. When soaking time is over, turn the machine back on and finish washing.

What happens if you add the clothes first, then the detergent and bleach?

Pouring detergent directly onto the clothes may prevent it from dissolving properly. This can inhibit its ability to clean your clothes. Another unhappy result can be residue or streaks of undissolved detergent on your "clean" clothes.

Pouring bleach directly onto the clothes can cause the color to fade. In the case of chlorine bleach, it can also weaken the fibers, creating holes or tears as the items are agitated in the wash cycle.

BLEACH TIME

If your clothes are particularly dingy, add chlorine bleach (if safe for the fabric) four to five minutes after the wash cycle starts. This gives the enzymes and optical brighteners in the detergent time to work. Be sure to use the machine's bleach dispenser so that you don't pour bleach directly onto the clothing. Note that all bleach, especially chlorine, has a limited shelf life: If you've had it longer than six months, it may not be doing its job properly.

Product Primer

Ever wonder what those ingredients listed on laundry product packages actually do?

ANTIREDEPOSITION AGENTS help prevent loosened soil from being redeposited onto fabrics as they go through the laundry cycles.

ENZYMES help break down complex protein stains and soils, such as grass and blood, so these stains can be more easily removed.

FRAGRANCES impart a pleasant scent to fabrics, reinforcing the idea that they are clean. Some detergents are offered in unscented versions, appealing to those who prefer little or no scent on their fabrics, or to those whose skin is sensitive to fragrance ingredients.

OXYGEN BLEACH is a nonchlorine bleach that maintains color and whiteness and can be used with most fabrics. If the item's care label says "Do Not Bleach" or has the "No Bleach" symbol, make sure your detergent does not have bleach as an additive.

PRESERVATIVES protect laundry products from the natural effects of product aging, such as decay, discoloration, oxidations, and bacterial attack. They also protect color and fragrance.

SODIUM CARBONATE provides alkalinity, which helps get clothes cleaner and softens the water.

SOLVENTS prevent ingredients in liquid laundry products from separating or disintegrating.

SURFACTANTS/CLEANING AGENTS improve the wetting ability of water and loosen and remove soil as the washing action takes place. As the soil is removed, it is emulsified, solubilized, or suspended in the wash solution until it is rinsed away.

Why Enzymes?

Enzymes are the darling of many laundry products, both prewash products and detergents. What makes them so great?

- Enzymes are a type of protein. They can be engineered to break down protein-, starch-, and fat-based stains. This makes them particularly effective on stains such as grass, blood, vomit, feces, oil, grease, perspiration, and milk.

- Enzymes work effectively at lower water temperatures and for a shorter amount of time, which conserves both water and energy.

- Enzymes are biodegradable.

Research indicates that proteases, a type of enzyme used in some detergents, can damage natural protein fibers, such as wool and silk. So for these fabrics, avoid detergents with enzymes unless the product label specifically states that it is safe to use on them.

Facts about Fabrics

Knowing the fiber content can help you determine the best method for cleaning an item and removing a stain. But in today's world of manufactured fibers, it can be almost impossible for the average person to determine the fiber content of an item. Polyesters masquerade as silks. Acrylics pretend to be wools. The soft, drapable fabric that the fashion world calls "challis" might be wool—or it might be rayon. A cotton shirt might actually be a cotton and polyester blend. And synthetic leather is sometimes difficult to distinguish from the real thing.

The first line of defense against this ambiguity is to save the fiber content and care instructions that come with textile items. These are generally permanently attached to the inside of garments. But for carpets, upholstery, bedspreads, comforters, and window treatments, this information either comes separately or is prominently attached to the outside of the item—a place most of us find unattractive, so we remove it...and then often lose it.

Therefore, it's a wise idea to develop some sort of filing system to keep track of this information. Easiest is a three-ring binder filled with top-loading plastic sheet protectors so that all care instructions can be conveniently organized, regardless of the size and format of the information. You can also tape this information to a laundry room wall.

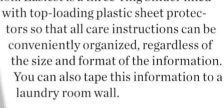

Three-ring binders are a perfect place to store care instructions for upholstery, bedspreads, comforters, and window treatments.

Why Can't I Wash This?

There are many reasons why an item might be marked "Dry-clean Only." Not all of them have to do with the main fabric. In the case of a garment, the outer fabric might be washable but the other fabrics (lining, interfacing, and so on) may not be. Or laundering might harm the buttons or the trim. If you want to try a do-it-yourself stain-removal technique, test the removal process first on an inconspicuous place on the item. If spotting, fiber melt, color change, or other signs of damage appear, take the item to a professional dry cleaner.

Leather Care

Many stain-removal techniques will damage leather. Some leathers are coated to resist staining; others are not. A special leather soap, which is spread onto the leather and then removed with a moist cloth, may remove some stains. However, some leather creams may create blotches. For greasy stains, an absorbent like cornmeal or talcum powder may do the trick. Check the leather manufacturer's care instructions and test the stain remover in an inconspicuous place on the item. If these techniques don't work, or if you're in doubt about how to care for your leather item, contact the manufacturer or look for a professional who specializes in cleaning leather.

Safety in the Laundry Room

- If there are small children or curious pets in your household, store all laundry products well out of their reach. Remember that little ones can climb and grab, so be sure to install childproof locks on cabinet doors. And don't leave open products unattended while you are doing the laundry.

- Never mix products that contain chlorine bleach with ammonia or with products that contain ammonia compounds, such as rust removers and some hand dishwashing detergents. Dangerous gases can be released.

- If you buy detergents or bleaches in large economy sizes and plan to repackage them in smaller containers for easy use, don't use any random container. It is safest to buy the same product in a smaller size and refill the container as needed. This way, the product is clearly labeled and the manufacturer's directions and precautions are always right at hand.

- For everyone's safety, program all phones (including cell phones) with the number for the Poison Control Center (800-222-1222).

Symbol Savvy

Some garment care labels consist of written instructions, some include symbols and written instructions, and others use just the symbols.

The chart on the opposite page shows the symbols and their meanings. Unless you have a very good memory, symbols-only labels can be very confusing! Why not make a copy of this chart, slip it into a plastic page protector, and post it in your laundry area?

Your Guide to Fabric Care Symbols

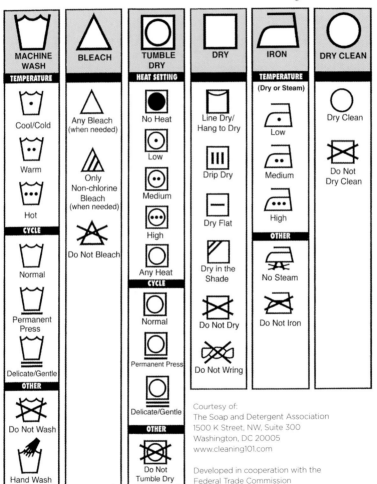

MACHINE WASH

TEMPERATURE

Cool/Cold

Warm

Hot

CYCLE

Normal

Permanent Press

Delicate/Gentle

OTHER

Do Not Wash

Hand Wash

BLEACH

Any Bleach (when needed)

Only Non-chlorine Bleach (when needed)

Do Not Bleach

TUMBLE DRY

HEAT SETTING

No Heat

Low

Medium

High

Any Heat

CYCLE

Normal

Permanent Press

Delicate/Gentle

OTHER

Do Not Tumble Dry

DRY

Line Dry/Hang to Dry

Drip Dry

Dry Flat

Dry in the Shade

Do Not Dry

Do Not Wring

IRON

TEMPERATURE (Dry or Steam)

Low

Medium

High

OTHER

No Steam

Do Not Iron

DRY CLEAN

Dry Clean

Do Not Dry Clean

Courtesy of:
The Soap and Detergent Association
1500 K Street, NW, Suite 300
Washington, DC 20005
www.cleaning101.com

Developed in cooperation with the
Federal Trade Commission

CLEANING GUIDE TO FIBERS AND FABRICS

Here is a general guide to choosing the right cleaning method for your garments. Care varies based on colorfastness, weight, trimmings, linings, special finishes, and fabric and garment construction. Always read and follow the manufacturer's care label recommendations before cleaning garments.

ACETATE Synthetic fiber. Dry-clean.

ACRYLIC Synthetic fiber. Machine wash knits in warm water on gentle setting. Wash inside out to reduce pilling. Roll in a towel to absorb extra moisture, and dry flat; or dry at low setting in a dryer. Dry-clean woven acrylic fabrics.

BLENDS Fabrics of combined fibers: cotton/polyester, cotton/linen, silk/polyester, wool/polyester, and so on. Follow care guidelines for the more delicate or most prominent fiber in the blend.

CANVAS Heavy, firm, tightly woven fabric, originally cotton or linen, now also made of synthetics or blends. Machine wash in cold water and tumble dry on low setting. Dry-clean if not colorfast.

CASHMERE Undercoat hair of the cashmere goat. Treat as wool, and follow the care label. Sweaters may be hand washed with care, but it's best to dry-clean both knits and wovens.

CHIFFON Thin, transparent fabric, usually silk; can be made of synthetic fibers. Hand wash for best results.

CHINTZ Glazed cotton, often printed. Dry-clean unless label states that glaze is durable and fabric can be washed; if so, wash as directed on labels.

CORDUROY Ridged-pile fabric that may be cotton, cotton/polyester, or rayon. Turn inside out and use warm water. Dry at regular setting; remove from dryer while slightly damp; smooth pockets and seams with hands. Hang until dry.

COTTON Natural vegetable fiber woven and knitted into fabrics of many weights and textures. Hand wash lightweight fabrics, such as batiste, organdy, and voile, and hang to air-dry (or iron damp with a hot iron). Machine wash light-colored and white medium- and heavyweight cottons with warm or hot water. Use cold water for bright colors that may bleed. Dry at regular or low setting. Remove from dryer while still damp. Iron damp with hot iron. Cottons like towels and underwear can be washed and dried on hot settings if desired.

DAMASK Jacquard-weave fabric; may be cotton, linen, silk, viscose, wool, or a blend. Hand wash lightweight fabrics (see individual fiber listings for care). Dry-clean silk, wool, and all heavier-weight fabrics.

DENIM Strong, heavy twill-weave fabric, usually cotton, but can be a cotton/synthetic blend. Prone to shrinkage unless purchased preshrunk. Machine wash in warm water. Traditional blue and other deep colors bleed the first several washings, so wash separately, as necessary. Dry at low setting to avoid shrinkage. Iron while damp with a hot iron, as needed.

DOWN Soft underplumage of water fowl, often combined with adult feathers (should be so labeled). Both machine-washable and dry-cleanable, but treatment depends on the fabric shell of the item; follow manufacturer's instructions carefully. Do not air-dry. Tumble dry on gentle setting (temperature no higher than 140°F or 60°C). Fluff and turn often during drying.

FLANNEL Napped fabric in plain or twill weave. Cotton and synthetics may be machine washed. Dry at low setting and remove while damp or line dry. Wool should be dry-cleaned.

GABARDINE Firm, closely woven twill fabric, often worsted wool; also made of cotton and synthetic fibers. Follow label directions or dry-clean.

LACE Open-work textile; may be cotton, linen, or synthetic. Hand wash using a detergent for delicate fabrics. Avoid rubbing. Squeeze out excess moisture; don't twist or wring. Shape by hand and hang to air-dry or dry flat; do not tumble dry. Pin delicate lace to a cloth before washing.

LINEN Natural flax fiber; light- to heavyweight fabrics. Hand wash or machine wash in warm water if colorfast; use oxygen bleach, as needed. Iron damp on wrong side. For heavy linens, use a hot iron; for lighter-weight linens, blends, and linens treated for crease resistance, use a lower temperature. Can also be dry-cleaned (especially heavy linens).

MICROFIBERS (IN CLEANING CLOTHS) Tightly woven polyester and nylon fibers. Machine wash separately to keep lint-free. Never use fabric softener, which reduces static properties and makes cleaning less effective. Line or machine dry on normal, again, separately from other laundry.

MICROFIBERS OR FLEECE (IN CLOTHING AND BEDDING)
Small and fine polyester yarns that are tightly woven. Machine wash in cool to moderately warm water and air dry or machine dry, warm setting. If you have not purchased anti-pill fabric, turn garments wrong side out when laundering to reduce pilling. Fleece is heat sensitive, so hot dryer temperatures and ironing should be avoided to reduce pilling.

MOHAIR Fiber from the angora goat. Treat as wool.

NYLON Synthetic fiber used in fabrics of different weights, sometimes blended with other fibers. When used alone, it is both dry-cleanable and machine-washable; use warm water. Tumble dry on a low setting, or hang on plastic hanger and drip- or air-dry. To avoid permanent yellowing, keep away from sunlight or direct heat.

ORGANDY Sheer, lightweight, plain weave cotton. Hand wash; starch to maintain characteristic crisp appearance. Iron damp with hot iron. Can also be dry-cleaned.

POLYESTER Strong synthetic fiber in fabrics of various weights and textures; often blended with cotton and wool. Does not shrink or stretch. Wash in warm water. Tumble dry and remove promptly to prevent wrinkles. Iron at low setting. If blended, follow guidelines for the more delicate fiber.

RAMIE Natural fiber from ramie plant (similar to linen), used alone or blended, often with cotton. Machine wash in warm water; tumble dry. Iron damp with hot iron. Can also be dry-cleaned. Avoid excessive twisting.

RAYON A generic term for a man-made fiber, including viscose and cuprammonium rayon. Some garment labels identify the fabric as "rayon," some as "viscose." Follow label care instructions. Dry-clean for best results.

RUBBER A fiber found in both natural and man-made form. Used in sneakers. Remove laces (wash those separately) and machine wash warm. For best results, air-dry or dry at low setting. Using too high a temperature in the dryer will sometimes melt the rubber or shrink the canvas part of the shoe.

SATIN Fabric with a lustrous finish, traditionally silk, now also acetate and polyester. Dry-clean silk and acetate. Wash polyester satins following fiber guidelines.

SEERSUCKER Fabric with puckered stripes woven in during the manufacturing process; usually cotton, but also nylon, polyester, and silk versions. See specific fiber for washing instructions. Drip or tumble dry. Iron on low heat, if needed.

SILK Natural fiber from the silkworm; in fabrics of various weights and textures. If recommended, hand wash plain-weave crepe de chine and thin, lightweight, and medium-weight silks in lukewarm water with mild soap or detergent or in cold water with special cold-water detergent. Do not use chlorine bleach. Rinse several times in cold water until no trace of suds remains; towel-blot. Dry flat. Iron on wrong side at warm (silk) setting. If so labeled, some silks can be machine washed; follow label directions carefully. Dry-clean heavier (suiting weight) silks, pleated silks, and those in dark colors, which may bleed.

SPANDEX Generic name for stretch fibers often added to other fibers to give them elasticity. Machine wash in warm water on the delicate cycle (if exercise wear, wash after each wearing to remove body oils, which can cause deterioration). Do not use chlorine bleach. Tumble dry on low setting. Iron using low setting.

TERRY CLOTH Toweling fabric with looped pile made of cotton or cotton/polyester. Machine wash in warm or hot water. Tumble dry or line dry.

VELOUR Napped fabric, originally wool, now also cotton, silk, and synthetics. Dry-clean unless manufacturer's label indicates it can be washed.

VELVET Soft-pile fabric, originally silk, now usually rayon or cotton. Dry-clean.

WOOL Natural fiber made of sheep fleece. Hand wash sweaters and other knits in cold water with cold-water detergent. Rinse thoroughly. Squeeze; do not wring. Towel-blot and dry flat, blocking back to original size. Machine-washable wools are so labeled; follow instructions carefully. Dry-clean woven wools and heavy sweaters.

two

First Aid
for Stains

When a stain requires more than basic laundry techniques, it's time for serious stain removal. There are several different ways to get rid of stains. The technique that works best will depend on the type of stain and where it's located. For example, if you spill a soft drink on your T-shirt, you can pretreat it with a stain-removal product and toss the shirt in the laundry. But if you spill the same soft drink on the carpet, you'll need to blot up the liquid, then apply the recommended stain remover (see Chapter 3), and blot some more.

Fabric comes into play, too. If the item is washable, you have more at-home treatment options than if it is dry-clean only. (Keep in mind, though, that some fibers react badly to the chemicals in some stain-removal products.) Obviously, it's important to have a good overview of the art of stain removal.

The Products

These are the products you're likely to need when you encounter stains. (Be aware that certain stains may set if not treated immediately.)

ABSORBENT Cornstarch, cornmeal, talcum power, or fuller's earth (which is available in pharmacies) can be used to absorb greasy stains.

ACETONE Use pure acetone or nonoily nail-polish remover on stains like nail polish or correction fluid. Do not use acetone on fabrics containing acetate or triacetate—it will melt these fibers! Be careful, too, on rayon, silk, and wool. Use with caution and in a well-ventilated area: Acetone is quite flammable and gives off fumes.

AMMONIA Purchase the household version of ammonia, which works well on dried blood, perspiration, citrus, juice, felt-tip pen, urine, and other acid-based stains. Note, however, that ammonia can damage silk and wool fibers. For stain-removal purposes, stay away from the sudsy or scented offerings. Test ammonia (and all stain removers) on an inconspicuous part of your fabric, carpet, or upholstery first, as it can cause some dyes to run. And never mix chlorine bleach and ammonia—the resulting fumes are hazardous.

BLEACH Keep two types on hand—chlorine and oxygen (all-fabric) bleach. Read the fabric-care label to determine which bleach is safe for your fabric. When in doubt, use the oxygen bleach. Never mix oxygen and chlorine bleach. When combined, they cancel each other out.

COLOR REMOVER Available where fabric dyes are sold, this product removes dye stains from whites that are washed by mistake with colored items. The Good Housekeeping Research Institute recommends Carbona Color Run Remover and Rit Color Remover.

DETERGENT For all-around stain removal on fabrics, choose a bleach-free liquid detergent with enzymes. For stain removal on upholstery and carpets, choose a bleach-free, lanolin-free liquid hand dishwashing detergent, such as Dawn or Joy. A useful formula for stain removal is one tablespoon of liquid laundry detergent or liquid hand dishwashing detergent dissolved in two cups of warm water. You can also rub full-strength liquid laundry detergent into stains. If you are treating a stain on an item that contains wool or silk fibers, do not use an enzyme detergent. Enzymes are "protein eaters," and these fibers are proteins.

DRY-CLEANING SOLVENT This is a generic term describing solvent-based liquids and sprays that are particularly useful for oily or greasy stains. One popular version is a powder that you spray on, let dry, and then brush off. Generally, dry-cleaning solvents are formulated for both dry-clean-only and washable fabrics, but read the product label to be sure. Some are specially formulated for specific types of stains, such as pet stains; others are formulated for specific textile categories. Many carpet cleaners and upholstery cleaners are dry-cleaning solvents.

Newer stain-removal products that are formulated just for upholstery—including dry-cleaning solvents—will include cleaning codes (W, S, and/or WS) on the label. If one of the codes on the label matches the code on your upholstery tag, you know that the product is safe to use. If you have misplaced or never had the upholstery cleaning code, test the cleaning method on a hidden spot or call a professional upholstery cleaner for advice.

With any dry-cleaning solvent, repeated light applications are more effective than one heavy dose. Always rinse out the solvent completely before laundering any item treated with solvent. The Good Housekeeping Research Institute recommends Afta Dry Cleaning Solvent and Spot Remover.

ENZYME PRESOAKS These products break down protein stains, such as blood, grass, and baby formula. A laundry detergent that contains enzymes can also be used for presoaking.

GLYCERIN Particularly useful for stains on carpets and upholstery, glycerin softens hardened stains. It is especially effective for mustard and curry stains, and is available in pharmacies.

HYDROGEN PEROXIDE This is useful for stubborn stains such as bird droppings, feces, and chocolate. Be sure to use a 3 percent solution of hydrogen peroxide, the type sold in pharmacies as a mild antiseptic.

DO NOT use the stronger solution that is sold for bleaching hair. Hydrogen peroxide is similar in function to oxygen bleach.

PAINT REMOVER Use the water-rinsable variety to soften hardened paint stains (both oil- and water-based). Paint remover is available where paint is sold.

PETROLEUM JELLY It softens hardened grease, tar, and oil stains.

PREWASH STAIN REMOVER Your favorite brand of stain remover is often the first line of defense against stains. But be sure to read the label, as the product may not be suitable for all fabrics. And there may be a recommended time frame for use. With stick versions, you can pretreat the item and then wait up to a week before washing; with spray versions, washing before the spray dries is recommended.

RUBBING ALCOHOL This is good for removing ballpoint ink, pencil, mascara, and colored candle-wax residue, even from drycleanables. Don't purchase rubbing alcohol with added color or fragrance; it may damage the fabric. When stronger action is required, purchase denatured or isopropyl alcohol, which is available in pharmacies. Note that these alcohols have a shelf life. Check the expiration date in order to get the most effective results.

RUST REMOVER Choose a commercial rust remover, available in supermarkets and hardware stores, or a 5 percent oxalic acid solution, which is available in pharmacies. Oxalic acid is poisonous, so always wear rubber gloves, rinse garments thoroughly to get rid of any traces of the rust remover, and avoid contact with skin and eyes. Always follow package directions carefully. The Good

Housekeeping Research Institute recommends Rit Rust Remover (for washable white fabrics) and Whink Rust Remover (for color-fast fabrics).

SODIUM THIOSULFATE Pure sodium thiosulfate, or "fixer," sold in pharmacies and photo-supply stores, is used to remove iodine and chlorine-bleach stains. Unless it is kept very tightly capped, this product has a shelf life of only a few months, so you will probably want to buy only on an "as-needed" basis.

Recommended by
THE GOOD HOUSEKEEPING RESEARCH INSTITUTE

There are many commercial stain-removal products designed to treat specific types of stains, often with varying degrees of success. But a few products have been consistently successful in tests conducted by the Good Housekeeping Research Institute:

- **Afta Dry Cleaning Solvent and Spot Remover:** for grease and oil-based stains.

- **Carbona Color Run Remover:** for removing unwanted dye stains from washable white and colorfast fabrics.

- **Red Erase from Evergreen Labs:** for removing "kid stains" caused by candy, liquid medicine, products with red dyes, and products with artificial colorings.

- **Rit Color Remover:** for removing unwanted dye stains from washable white fabrics.

- **Rit Rust Remover:** for removing rust stains from washable white fabrics.

- **Whink Rust Remover:** for removing rust stains from colorfast fabrics.

- **Wine Away from Evergreen Labs:** for removing red-wine stains, as well as stains caused by grape juice, coffee, pet accidents, and grease.

VINEGAR AND DYE

White vinegar may change the color of some dyes. If a color change occurs after using white vinegar, rinse or sponge well with clear water to remove the vinegar. Apply a few drops of ammonia (caution, see page 33) and then rinse or sponge again with clear water. This may restore the fabric's original color.

WATERLESS HAND CLEANER Use a waterless hand cleaner, sold in grocery stores and drugstores, as a prewash for stubborn oil and grease stains. Work the cleaner into the fabric and remove it with warm water.

WHITE VINEGAR This is the only variety of vinegar that can be used for stain removal. The others will add stains, not take them away! White vinegar is particularly effective on old perspiration stains and for neutralizing pet stains and odors on carpets or upholstery. It can also help restore color that has been damaged by the stain itself or by the treatment process.

The Tools

Stain removal doesn't require a lot of elaborate tools. Here's pretty much all you will need.

BRUSHES A flat, medium-bristle brush and/or a collection of old toothbrushes, as well as a soft-bristle clothes brush.

COTTON SWABS Use cotton swabs when you want to apply a small amount of stain-removal product to an inconspicuous place on a garment, upholstery, or carpet to test its reaction with the fabric.

CLUB SODA AND STAINS

Although many people swear by club soda as a stain remover, there seems to be no scientific basis for its popularity. The fact that it is generally right at hand, so that the stain is treated promptly, probably accounts for its success. Plain tap water is cheaper and works just as well.

WHITE CLOTHS One hundred percent cotton cloths are the most absorbent when blotting stains, but cotton/poly blends will work well, too. Save your old T-shirts and worn-out towels. They'll do a great job on fresh stains.

PAPER TOWELS Use plain white paper towels for blotting—no colors or prints.

EYEDROPPER This handy tool lets you put a small amount of stain-removal solution exactly where you need it.

SPRAY BOTTLE Useful for applying cleaning solutions, such as detergent and water, to carpets and upholstery. A spray bottle lets you control the amount of moisture without overwetting the item.

SQUEEZE BOTTLE This tool works like an eyedropper but is designed for bigger jobs.

FABRIC DOS AND DON'TS

Not all fabrics take kindly to every type of laundry or stain-removal product.

COTTON

- Don't use chlorine bleach or fabric softener on children's cotton nightclothes. Both of these substances will harm the flame-retardant finish, which is mandated by law for children's sleepwear.

- Vinegar, with its high degree of acidity, can be harmful to cotton. If you use it for stain removal, sponge the stain with the vinegar solution, then wash the item immediately.

SILK

- Don't use acetone.
- Don't use chlorine bleach.
- If the silk is washable, avoid detergent with enzymes. Use a mild liquid hand dishwashing detergent or a product specially formulated for silks; baby shampoo is a great substitute.
- Don't use prewash stain removers with enzymes.

SPANDEX

- Don't use chlorine bleach on anything with spandex fibers. It will destroy the elasticity.

WOOL

- Most wools are dry-clean only; some (particularly wool knits) can be gently hand washed and air-dried. Check the care label.
- If the wool is washable, avoid detergents with enzymes. Use a mild liquid hand dishwashing detergent or a product specially formulated for washing wool—or try baby shampoo instead.
- Don't use prewash stain removers with enzymes.

The Techniques

These ten stain-removal techniques are designed with three goals in mind: (1) to dislodge the stain from the fabric; (2) to avoid grinding the stain deeper into the fibers; and (3) to treat the fabric gently so it retains its original look and feel. (Each stain in Chapter 3, "The A-to-Z Stain-Removal Guide," will tell you which specific technique to use for which stain and which surface.)

Here are all the stain-removal techniques you need to know.

BLOT To lift out stains, saturate the area with stain remover. Wait one minute, and then blot with a clean white cloth or paper towel. To keep the stain from spreading, begin blotting at the stain's outer edge and work toward the center. Blot in an uneven pattern around the edge of the stain so you won't leave a ring when the fabric, carpet, or upholstery dries. You can also use this technique to remove the excess stain before applying the stain remover.

BRUSH Using a medium-bristle brush, gently flick the particles up and away from the fabric (like brushing crumbs off a table). For small areas, an old toothbrush works fine.

For dry, caked-on substances like mud and mildew, the goal is to remove the excess before treating the actual stain. A handheld vacuum works well to remove excess dry mud or flower-pollen stains without pushing them into the fabric. (See Vacuum, page 42.)

If you are using an absorbent—such as cornstarch or talcum powder—to remove a greasy stain, apply the product, let it sit a few minutes to absorb the stain, then gently brush away the residue.

On carpets and upholstery, brush first, before using any other method, to break up and remove as much dry material as possible. Vacuum up the residue before proceeding with the next stain-removal step.

FLUSH With this technique, the stain is removed by transferring it from one surface to another. Start by putting a clean absorbent pad or a layer of paper towels, folded and refolded to at least a 1/8-inch thickness, underneath the spot. Using an eyedropper, a squeeze bottle, or a spray bottle, apply the flushing agent slowly so it is absorbed into the pad, taking some of the stain with it. Change the pad as soon as you see traces of the stain. In some instances, flushing is done by holding the stained fabric under the faucet and letting the tap water rush through it.

FREEZE This is usually the first step in removing soft, pliable, or gooey substances like chewing gum, rubber cement, and candle wax. Apply either cold water or an ice cube wrapped in small plastic bag to the stain. If the stained item is small enough, you can even pop it in the freezer for a few minutes. The goal is to harden the substance so most of it can be scraped off before additional treatment.

PRESOAK This is an effective way to loosen heavy soils prior to laundering. You can do it in a basin, in the sink, or even in the washing machine. Of course, you need more than water for effective soaking! Choices include detergent, bleach, or a laundry product specifically designed for presoaking. Mix the soaking agent with water, and then add the item(s) to be soaked. Minimal soaking time is 30 minutes; maximum is usually overnight. (Longer and you run the risk of damaging the fabric's color.) If you are dealing with protein-based stains (such as blood or egg), choose a product with enzymes. But don't mix a detergent or presoak containing enzymes with chlorine bleach. The chlorine will deactivate the enzymes.

PRETREAT This term refers to applying a stain-removal product directly on individual spots or stains prior to washing. Products specifically formulated for stain removal come in spray, liquid, or stick form. But you can also make your own pretreatment product by mixing granular detergent and water to form a paste and rubbing it into the spot. Liquid laundry detergent or a bar of soap can also be used to pretreat stains.

SCRAPE For 3-D stains (think baby food, eggs, chocolate, melted crayon), the goal is to get rid of the excess before attacking the stain itself. Use a dull knife or the back of a spoon to gently remove the excess without harming the fabric, carpet, or upholstery.

SPONGE Place the stained item right side up over an absorbent pad. Using a clean white cloth dampened with the stain-removal product, gently dab the area so the stain migrates out of the fabric and onto the pad. To prevent restaining the area, change the absorbent pad frequently. Sponging with clear water may also be used as a final step to "rinse" other stain-removal products from upholstery and carpeting.

TAMP Tamping is a particularly effective technique for carpet and upholstery stains. It's an up-and-down motion using a brush with bristles that are the same length. The goal is to break up the stain. Don't confuse tamping with scrubbing. Scrubbing is a back-and-forth motion that may grind the stain further into the item.

VACUUM When you need to get fine particles like pollen off the fabric, carpet, or upholstery while avoiding the risk of grinding them in further, then it's time to pull out the vacuum cleaner. In the case of mold and mildew, vacuuming is the alternative solution when it isn't possible to take the item outdoors for a good brushing.

Putting It All Together: Getting Rid of Those Stains

The easiest way to find out how to treat a stain is to refer to Chapter 3, "The A-to-Z Stain-Removal Guide." But what if your particular stain isn't listed? Here's what to do.

1 Look for a similar stain.

For example, stains caused by ziti with tomato sauce are treated the same way as spaghetti-sauce stains. When looking for a similar stain, remember that stains are often categorized into types. Once you find the type of stain you have, simply follow the appropriate stain-removal techniques. Here are the types of stains.

- *Protein stains.* This category includes baby food, baby formula, blood, cheese, cream, egg, feces, gelatin, ice cream, milk, mud, vomit, white glue, and urine.

- *Oil-based stains.* This category includes automotive oil, bacon, butter, body oils (collar and cuff soil), cooking oil, hair oil, hand lotion, margarine, mayonnaise, and salad dressing.

- *Tannin stains.* This category includes alcoholic beverages, some berries (cranberries, raspberries, and strawberries), grapes, coffee, fruit juice, perfume, soft drinks, tea, and tomato juice.

- *Dye stains.* This category includes blueberries, cherries, curry, food coloring, grass, hair dye, ink, iodine, Mercurochrome, and mustard.

- *Combination stains.* This category includes coffee with cream, chocolate ice cream, cosmetics, crayons, and shoe polish.

2 Check out the ingredients listed on the label of the product that caused the stain.

Look for clues to handling the stain:

- Many products contain dyes. If you find a listing for "FD&C" followed by a color name and number, it is a dye that is safe for food, drugs, and cosmetics. Check out the techniques listed for Food Coloring stains on pages 124–125. If the dye is listed as "D&C" and followed by a color name and number, it is a dye that is safe only for drugs and cosmetics. Check out the techniques listed for Hair Dye stains on page 145.

- Some over-the-counter cough, cold, and flu medications contain alcohol; others do not. Anything formulated for children should not contain alcohol. Use the stain-removal techniques under Cough Syrup on page 98 for those stains. If the adult medication contains alcohol (read the product label), treat the stain as for Medicine, Alcohol-based, on page 173.

3 Ask the manufacturer.

You may be able to find the manufacturer's phone number or website on the package. Or you can conduct an Internet search by the product name. This will probably take you to the manufacturer's website, where you will find information on how to contact them by e-mail and/or phone. The website may also contain stain-removal information for their products.

4 Treat it as a mystery stain.

If you've identified the stain but still have no clue what to do about it, this is a mystery stain! Follow the procedures on page 75, "Treating Mystery Stains."

Upholstery and Carpets

As you use "The A-to-Z Stain-Removal Guide," you'll note that we've separated the stain treatments into three categories: fabric, upholstery, and carpet. Although we tend to lump both upholstered items and carpeting into the same "home furnishings" category, they don't always have the same fiber content. And fiber content can be an important factor in determining how stains are treated.

How Are They Different?

Upholstery fabrics contain a wide range of fibers. The list of commonly used fibers includes linen, cotton, wool, silk, acetate, acrylic, rayon, and polypropelene (commonly called olefin). These fibers may be used alone or in blends. Polyester and nylon are found in upholstery fabrics, too, but they are almost always blended with other fibers.

The fiber range of carpets is much narrower. The four common fibers are nylon, olefin, polyester, and wool. Cotton fibers are occasionally used in area rugs. Silk fibers can be found in some very high-end Oriental carpets, but carpets containing silk should always be professionally cleaned. Acetate is never used for carpets.

So the bad news is that you have to be more careful about how you treat stains on upholstered items. With so many fiber possibilities, paired with the fact that many upholstered items have been around for a long time and are no longer or never were labeled for fiber content, it's often impossible to know what you are dealing with. But there's good news, too! An upholstered item usually offers more inconspicuous places to test a stain-removal technique than a carpet does—and "The A-to-Z Stain-Removal Guide" will help you determine exactly which technique is best for both.

Upholstery Cleaning Codes

The furniture industry has developed voluntary codes that indicate the appropriate cleaning methods for upholstery. If the manufacturer of your furniture used these codes, you'll find them printed on fabric samples, on a label under seat cushions, or on hangtags. Use these labels as a guide to spot removal and for overall cleaning. If no code exists, try a cleaning method on a hidden spot or call a professional upholstery cleaner for advice.

W Clean the fabric with a water-based product, such as the foam from a mild detergent or an upholstery shampoo. Use sparingly and avoid overwetting.

S Clean the fabric with a mild water-free dry-cleaning solvent. Check the list of contents on the label. Use sparingly, in a well-ventilated room.

WS Clean the fabric with a dry-cleaning solvent, the foam of a mild detergent, or an upholstery shampoo, depending on the stain.

X Have the fabric professionally cleaned. Clean this fabric yourself only by vacuuming or brushing it lightly to prevent accumulation of dust and grime.

Carpet Cautions

- Many carpets come with care information. When you purchase a new carpet, put this information in a safe place so you can find it when you need it.

- Many of today's carpets are treated with stain-resistant finishes. However, this doesn't mean that you will never need to worry about stain removal! A stain-resistant finish simply holds the spill on the fiber's surface. This gives you some time to blot up the spill and use the appropriate stain-removal technique before the stain has a chance to penetrate the fibers. The longer you leave the spill unattended, however, the more difficult it will be to remove.

- If you've invested in a very expensive carpet, be especially cautious about treating stains yourself. Call in a carpet-cleaning professional.

- If possible, put a cloth towel under the area where you are working to avoid spreading moisture to the carpet pad and/or the floor.

- Avoid overwetting the carpet.

- Once you have removed the stain from the carpet, cover the damp spot with a stack of paper towels (at least $1/8$ inch thick). Weight down with a heavy object, such as a vase or pot, and leave overnight. As the carpet dries, any residue that remains from the stain will be absorbed into the paper towels. The next day, remove the paper towels and fluff up the carpet with your hands or a soft brush.

TWELVE GOLDEN RULES OF FABRIC STAIN REMOVAL

1 **Identify the stain** No clue what it is? See "The Stain with No Name," page 50. Using the wrong treatment increases the risk of setting the stain permanently. A safe solution is to rinse or soak the garment in cold water before laundering or applying a stain remover.

2 **Read the care label** Knowing whether the item is dry-clean only or the type of bleach to use will save you time and heartache.

3 **Stock up** Since quick treatment increases your rate of success, keep your laundry room well stocked with the tools and supplies listed in this chapter.

4 **Check for colorfastness** If you're not sure the color will run, use an eyedropper or a cotton swab to apply the recommended stain remover to an inconspicuous spot (a seam allowance, hem allowance, the underside of the sofa cushion, and so on). Rinse or sponge with cold water and let dry. If there's no color change or water spotting, continue with the treatment. If the color is damaged, consult a dry cleaner.

5 **Don't delay** The fresher the stain, the better your chances of getting it out.

6 **Soak the stain** This is the easiest way to loosen heavy soils. Soak in cool water anywhere from 30 minutes to overnight (depending on the type of stain, how heavy the soil is, and how much time you have).

7 Prewash This is an alternative to soaking. You're actually running the wash and spin cycles twice, with water extraction but no rinsing in between. This prolongs the agitation that removes greasy or heavy soil. Some washing machines have a prewash cycle that includes a short soak period; others require you to set the controls manually. Check your appliance instructions to be sure. Use detergent or a presoak product in the first wash cycle; add detergent again for the second wash cycle.

8 Pretreat difficult stains Don't rely on the washing machine to do all the work. In the best-case scenario, you completely remove the stain before the item is laundered.

9 Be prepared No laundry room nearby? No problem! Stain sticks are easy to take along wherever you go. Stash them in convenient places like glove compartments, diaper bags, beach totes, and carry-on luggage. These products are especially effective on polyester fibers and oil-based stains, and can usually be left on the fabric for up to a week.

10 Check before drying Never put an item in the dryer until the stain is completely removed. Otherwise, the heat of the dryer will permanently set the stain.

11 Be patient You may have to repeat a treatment several times before the stain completely disappears.

12 Launder If the item is washable, always launder it after using a stain-removal product.

The Stain with No Name

Remember the children's game of "Who Am I?" where you guessed an identity by asking questions that could be answered only by "yes" or "no"? Stains can play the "Who Am I?" game, too.

And why is it best to know what the stain is? Well, the "just treat 'em all the same" philosophy will work most of the time, but why run the risk of doing something that might set the stain permanently—or waste your time trying lots of alternatives? When the origin of a stain has you stumped, here are a few things to consider.

1 Check the location. Food stains tend to be on the front of a garment and are generally protein stains.

2 Search your memory. What were you doing when you last wore this garment? Or what did you serve your guests that was likely to spill on the carpet?

3 Scratch and sniff. Stains like alcohol, fruit juice, perfume, and motor oil have distinct odors.

4 Observe the color. This can be tricky. For example, rust stains can appear similar to tea or coffee stains, but treating them the wrong way may set them permanently. Other stains can get paler over time. And the benzoyl peroxide that's an ingredient in some cosmetics can cause color loss. That's why it's important to search your memory!

If you still have no clue as to the origin of the stain, check out "Treating Mystery Stains" on page 75.

DRY-CLEANING KITS: YES OR NO?

In-home dry-cleaning kits are an economical solution for removing odors and light stains from dry-clean-only items. As a result, they also help extend the time between dry cleanings. For heavily soiled or stained items, put the money you would have spent on the kit toward the services of a professional dry cleaner.

three

The A-to-Z Stain-Removal Guide

ThIS chapter is an easy-to-use guide—in alphabetical order—to removing more than 80 stains. Under each stain entry, the directions are broken down into three categories. Here's why.

FABRIC When you are treating a stain on fabric, you have full access to the stain. You can treat it from the front, you can treat it from the back, you can sponge it, you can soak it, you can launder it—in short, as long as the fabric is washable, you can do pretty much whatever it takes to remove that stain.

UPHOLSTERY In order to treat a stain on upholstery, you have to work on the surface of the fabric. Soaking and laundering aren't options; techniques like blotting and sponging are better choices. In addition, when it comes to upholstery fabrics, there are many fiber possibilities. New upholstery may have labeling for fiber content and a care code. However, many upholstered items have been around for a long time; they either are no longer labeled with fiber content and care codes or never were. Conservative methods are called for because you may not know which fiber(s) you have. Try the recommended cleaning method on a hidden spot. If it doesn't work, or if you are unsure about its safety for your fabric, call a professional upholstery cleaner for advice.

CARPET Unless it's an area rug that you can lift up, the same stain limitations apply to carpet as to upholstery. Then why not just lump upholstery and carpet together? Because carpets are generally made of nylon, olefin, polyester, or wool fibers, either alone or in combination with each other. Carpets don't contain unusual or unknown fibers. The information in this chapter is cross-referenced with the information in Chapter 2.

> When you are treating a stain on fabric, you have full access to the stain. As long as the fabric is washable, you can do pretty much whatever it takes to remove that stain.

Before you attack your stain, go back to Chapter 2 and review techniques and products. Doing things the right way with the right product will give you better results. Note that references to ammonia and acetone in this A-to-Z section are followed by a caution that sends you back to Chapter 2; refer to this information before treating your stain. Finally, know when it's time to call in reinforcements. If you're not making any progress with a stain, STOP!

- For carpets and upholstery, call in an upholstery- or carpet-cleaning professional.
- Let a washable item air-dry. DO NOT put it in the dryer; the heat of the dryer can permanently set the stain. Take it to a dry cleaner. Explain what the stain is and what you have done to try to remove it.

ALCOHOLIC BEVERAGES

FABRIC

1 Sponge the stain with cool water or soak for about 30 minutes in a basin of cool water.
2 Pretreat with a prewash stain remover.
3 Launder. If it's safe for the fabric, add chlorine bleach to the wash.

UPHOLSTERY

method 1

1 Mix one tablespoon of white vinegar with 2/3 cup of rubbing alcohol.
2 Using a clean white cloth, sponge the stain with the vinegar-alcohol solution.
3 Blot until the liquid is absorbed.
4 Repeat Steps 2 and 3 until the stain disappears.

method 2

1 Mix one tablespoon of liquid hand dishwashing detergent with two cups of cool water.
2 Using a clean white cloth, sponge the stain with the detergent solution.
3 Blot until the liquid is absorbed.
4 Repeat Steps 2 and 3 until the stain disappears.
5 Sponge with cold water and blot dry to remove the detergent solution.

CARPET

1 Using clean white paper towels or cloths, blot up as much of the spilled beverage as possible.
2 Use plain water or mix one tablespoon of liquid hand dishwashing detergent and one tablespoon of white vinegar with two cups of warm water.
3 Using a clean white cloth, sponge the stain with a small amount of plain water or detergent-vinegar solution. Apply a little bit at a time, blotting frequently with a dry cloth until the stain disappears.
4 If using a detergent-vinegar solution, sponge with cold water and blot dry to remove the solution.

APPLE JUICE OR APPLESAUCE

FABRIC

1 If applesauce, scrape off excess fruit.
2 Flush under cold running water.
3 Launder, using the warmest water and type of bleach safe for the fabric.

UPHOLSTERY

1 If applesauce, scrape
off excess fruit;
vacuum up any residue.

2 Mix one tablespoon of
liquid hand dishwashing
detergent with two cups of cool water.

3 Using a clean white cloth, sponge the stain
with the detergent solution.

4 Blot until the liquid is absorbed.

5 Repeat Steps 3 and 4 until the stain disappears.

6 Sponge with cold water and blot dry to remove the
detergent solution.

CARPET

1 If applesauce, scrape off excess fruit; vacuum up any residue.

2 Mix one tablespoon of liquid hand dishwashing detergent with
two cups of warm water.

3 Using a clean white cloth, sponge the stain with the solution.

4 Blot until the liquid is absorbed.

5 Repeat Steps 3 and 4 until the stain disappears or is no longer
absorbed into the cloth.

6 If the stain remains, mix one tablespoon of ammonia (caution,
see page 33) with two cups of warm water.

7 Sponge the stain with the ammonia solution. Blot until the liquid
is absorbed.

8 Repeat Step 7 until the stain disappears.

9 Sponge with cold water and blot dry.

ASH

FABRIC

1 Pretreat with a prewash stain remover.
2 Launder, using the warmest water and type of bleach safe for the fabric.
3 If the stain remains, sponge with rubbing alcohol and launder again.

UPHOLSTERY

method 1

1 Sponge the stain with a clean white cloth and dry-cleaning solvent.
2 Blot until the solvent is absorbed.
3 Repeat Steps 1 and 2 until the stain disappears.

method 2

1 Mix one tablespoon of liquid hand dishwashing detergent with two cups of cool water.
2 Using a clean white cloth, sponge the stain with the detergent solution.
3 Blot until the liquid is absorbed.
4 Repeat Steps 2 and 3 until the stain disappears.
5 Sponge with cold water and blot dry to remove the detergent solution.

CARPET

1 Sprinkle baking soda, cornstarch, or other absorbent on the stain. Let stand at least one hour, and then vacuum.
2 Sponge the stain with a clean white cloth and a dry-cleaning solvent.
3 Blot until the solvent is absorbed.
4 Repeat Steps 2 and 3 until the stain disappears.
5 Sponge the carpet to remove the solvent and blot until the liquid is absorbed.

AVOCADO

FABRIC

1 Scrape off excess avocado.
2 Flush under cold running water to loosen the stain.
3 Pretreat with a prewash stain remover.
4 Launder, using the hottest water and type of bleach safe for the fabric.

UPHOLSTERY

1 Scrape off excess avocado.
2 Mix one tablespoon of liquid hand dishwashing detergent with two cups of cool water.
3 Using a clean white cloth, sponge the stain with the solution.
4 Blot until the liquid is absorbed.
5 Repeat Steps 3 and 4 until the stain disappears.
6 Sponge with cold water and blot dry.

CARPET

1 Scrape off excess avocado.
2 Mix one tablespoon of liquid hand dishwashing detergent with two cups of warm water.
3 Using a clean white cloth, sponge the stain with the solution.
4 Blot until the liquid is absorbed.
5 Repeat Steps 3 and 4 until the stain disappears or is no longer absorbed into the cloth.
6 If the stain remains, mix one tablespoon of ammonia (caution, see page 33) with two cups of warm water.
7 Sponge the stain with the ammonia solution. Blot until the liquid is absorbed.
8 Repeat Step 7 until the stain disappears.
9 Sponge with cold water and blot dry.

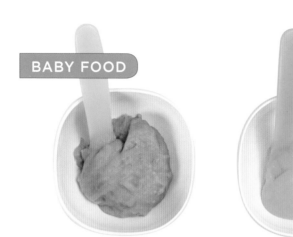

BABY FOOD

Use these removal techniques for mixed-ingredient baby foods, such as "assorted vegetables." For single-ingredient baby foods, such as "carrots," consult the appropriate stain-removal entry.

FABRIC

1 Presoak in cold water and liquid laundry detergent.
2 Launder in warm water.
3 If the stains remain, pretreat with a prewash stain remover or rub liquid laundry detergent into the stain.
4 Launder again.

UPHOLSTERY

method 1

1 Using a clean white cloth, sponge the stain with a dry-cleaning solvent.
2 Blot until the solvent is absorbed.
3 Repeat Steps 1 and 2 until the stain disappears.

method 2

1 Mix one tablespoon of liquid hand dishwashing detergent with two cups of cool water.

2 Using a clean white cloth, sponge the stain with the detergent solution.

3 Blot until the liquid is absorbed.

4 Repeat Steps 2 and 3 until the stain disappears.

5 Sponge with cold water and blot dry.

....

CARPET

method 1

1 Using a clean white cloth, sponge the stain with a dry-cleaning solvent.

2 Blot until the solvent is absorbed.

3 Repeat Steps 1 and 2 until the stain disappears.

4 Sponge with cold water and blot dry.

method 2

1 Mix one tablespoon of liquid hand dishwashing detergent with two cups of warm water.

2 Using a clean white cloth, sponge the stain with the detergent solution.

3 Blot until the liquid is absorbed.

4 Repeat Steps 2 and 3 until the stain disappears.

5 Sponge with cold water and blot dry.

BABY FORMULA → SEE FORMULA

BABY OIL

FABRIC

1 Pretreat with a prewash stain remover.
2 Launder, using the hottest water safe for the fabric.

UPHOLSTERY

1 Sprinkle baking soda, cornstarch, or other absorbent on the stain. Let stand 10 to 15 minutes, and then vacuum.
2 Using a clean white cloth, sponge the stain with a dry-cleaning solvent.
3 Blot until the solvent is absorbed.
4 Repeat Steps 2 and 3 until the stain disappears.

CARPET

1 If possible, scrape off excess oil.
2 Sprinkle baking soda, cornstarch, or other absorbent on the stain. Let stand 10 to 15 minutes, and then vacuum.
3 Using a clean white cloth, sponge the stain with a dry-cleaning solvent.
4 Blot until the solvent is absorbed.
5 Repeat Steps 3 and 4 until the stain disappears or is no longer absorbed into the cloth.
6 If the stain remains, mix one tablespoon of liquid hand dishwashing detergent and one tablespoon of white vinegar with two cups of warm water. Sponge the stain with this solution. Blot until the liquid is absorbed.
7 Sponge with cold water and blot dry to remove the detergent-vinegar solution.

BAKED BEANS

FABRIC

1 Scrape off excess baked beans.

2 Working from the back of the stain, flush with cold water.

3 Pretreat with a liquid laundry detergent, tamp the stain, and let stand for several minutes.

4 Rinse well.

5 Sponge with white vinegar, and then rinse well.

6 Repeat Steps 3 through 5 until you have removed as much stain as possible.

7 Pretreat with a prewash stain remover, and then launder.

8 If the stain remains, rub with a liquid laundry detergent, and then soak in warm water for up to 30 minutes.

9 Launder.

UPHOLSTERY

1 Scrape off excess baked beans.

2 Mix one tablespoon of liquid hand dishwashing detergent with two cups of cool water.

3 Using a clean white cloth, sponge the stain with the detergent solution.

4 Blot until the liquid is absorbed.

5 Repeat Steps 3 and 4 until the stain disappears.

6 Sponge with cold water and blot dry.

CARPET

1 Scrape off excess baked beans.
2 Mix one tablespoon of liquid hand dishwashing detergent with two cups of warm water.
3 Using a clean white cloth, sponge the stain with the detergent solution.
4 Blot until the liquid is absorbed.
5 Repeat Steps 3 and 4 until the stain disappears or is no longer absorbed into the cloth.
6 If the stain remains, mix one tablespoon of ammonia (caution, see page 33) with $1/2$ cup of warm water.
7 Sponge the stain with the ammonia solution.
8 Blot until the liquid is absorbed.
9 Sponge with cold water and blot dry.

BANANA

FABRIC

1 Scrape off excess banana.
2 Flush under cold running water.
3 Launder, using the warmest water and type of bleach safe for the fabric.

UPHOLSTERY

1 Scrape off excess banana.
2 Mix one tablespoon of liquid hand dishwashing detergent with two cups of cool water.
3 Using a clean white cloth, sponge the stain with the detergent solution.
4 Blot until the liquid is absorbed.
5 Repeat Steps 3 and 4 until the stain disappears.
6 Sponge with cold water and blot dry.

CARPET

1 Scrape off excess banana.

2 Mix one tablespoon of liquid hand dishwashing detergent with two cups of warm water.

3 Using a clean white cloth, sponge the stain with the detergent solution.

4 Blot until the liquid is absorbed.

5 Repeat Steps 3 and 4 until the stain disappears or is no longer absorbed into the cloth.

6 If the stain remains, mix one tablespoon of ammonia (caution, see page 33) with two cups of warm water.

7 Sponge the stain with the ammonia solution.

8 Blot until the liquid is absorbed.

9 Sponge with cold water and blot dry.

BARBECUE SAUCE

FABRIC

1 Working from the back of the stain, flush with cold water.

2 Pretreat with a liquid laundry detergent, tamp the stain, and let stand for several minutes.

3 Rinse well.

4 Sponge the stain with white vinegar, and then rinse well.

5 Repeat Steps 2 through 4 until you have removed as much stain as possible.

6 Pretreat with a prewash stain remover, and then launder with bleach that's safe for the fabric.

7 If the stain remains, rub with a liquid laundry detergent, and then soak in warm water for up to 30 minutes.

8 Launder.

....

UPHOLSTERY

1 Mix one tablespoon of liquid hand dishwashing detergent with two cups of cool water.
2 Using a clean white cloth, sponge the stain with the detergent solution.
3 Blot until the liquid is absorbed.
4 Repeat Steps 2 and 3 until the stain disappears.
5 Sponge with cold water and blot dry.

....

CARPET

1 Mix one tablespoon of liquid hand dishwashing detergent with two cups of warm water.
2 Using a clean white cloth, sponge the stain with the detergent solution.
3 Blot until the liquid is absorbed.
4 Repeat Steps 2 and 3 until the stain disappears or is no longer absorbed into the cloth.
5 If the stain remains, mix one tablespoon of ammonia (caution, see page 33) with $1/2$ cup of warm water.
6 Sponge the stain with the ammonia solution.
7 Blot until the liquid is absorbed.
8 Sponge with cold water and blot dry.

BEER

FABRIC

1 Sponge the spot with cool water or soak for about 30 minutes in a basin of cool water.
2 Pretreat with a prewash stain remover.
3 Launder. If it's safe for the fabric, add chlorine bleach to the wash.

UPHOLSTERY

method 1

1 Using clean white paper towels or cloths, blot up as much of the spilled beer as possible.

2 Mix one tablespoon of white vinegar with $2/3$ cup of rubbing alcohol.

3 Using a clean white cloth, sponge the stain with the vinegar-alcohol solution.

4 Blot until the liquid is absorbed.

5 Repeat Steps 3 and 4 until the stain disappears.

6 Sponge with cold water and blot dry.

method 2

1 Using clean white paper towels or cloths, blot up as much of the spilled beer as possible.

2 Mix one tablespoon of liquid hand dishwashing detergent with two cups of cool water.

3 Using a clean white cloth, sponge the stain with the detergent solution.

4 Blot until the liquid is absorbed.

5 Repeat Steps 3 and 4 until the stain disappears.

6 Sponge with cold water and blot dry.

CARPET

1 Using clean white paper towels or cloths, blot up as much of the spilled beer as possible.

2 Use warm plain water or mix one tablespoon of liquid hand dishwashing detergent and one tablespoon of white vinegar with two cups of warm water.

3 Sponge the stain with plain water or the detergent-vinegar solution. Apply a little bit at a time, blotting frequently with a dry cloth until the stain disappears.

4 If using a detergent-vinegar solution, sponge with cold water and blot dry to remove the solution.

BEETS

FABRIC

1 Pretreat with liquid laundry detergent or a prewash stain remover, and then rinse well with cold water.

2 If the stain remains, soak in a solution of cold water and chlorine or oxygen bleach. Chlorine bleach is preferable if it is safe for the fabric.

3 Launder in cold water with fabric-appropriate bleach, if needed.

UPHOLSTERY

1 Mix one tablespoon of liquid hand dishwashing detergent with two cups of cool water.

2 Using a clean white cloth, sponge the stain with the detergent solution.

3 Blot until the liquid is absorbed.

4 Repeat Steps 2 and 3 until the stain disappears or is no longer absorbed into the cloth.

5 If the stain remains, mix one tablespoon of ammonia (caution, see page 33) with $1/2$ cup of cool water.

6 Sponge the stain with the ammonia solution.

7 Blot until the liquid is absorbed.

8 Sponge with cold water and blot dry.

— Worth a Try —

If the beet stain is fresh, try blotting it with a piece of white bread to absorb some of the liquid.

CARPET

1 Mix one tablespoon of liquid hand dishwashing detergent with two cups of warm water.

2 Using a clean white cloth, sponge the stain with the detergent solution.

3 Blot until the liquid is absorbed.

4 Repeat Steps 2 and 3 until the stain disappears or is no longer absorbed into the cloth.

5 If the stain remains, mix one tablespoon of ammonia (caution, see page 33) with $1/2$ cup of warm water.

6 Sponge the stain with the ammonia solution.

7 Blot until the liquid is absorbed.

8 Sponge with cold water and blot dry.

BIRD DROPPINGS

FABRIC

1 Pretreat or soak in warm water with a laundry product containing enzymes.

2 Launder.

3 If the stain remains, use an eyedropper to apply hydrogen peroxide, and then apply a drop or two of ammonia (caution, see page 33). Flush with water.

4 Launder again.

BIRDS AND BERRIES

If the bird droppings are dark like berry stains, treat them as a blueberry stain (see page 72).

UPHOLSTERY

1 Mix one tablespoon of liquid hand dishwashing detergent with two cups of cool water.

2 Using a clean white cloth, sponge the stain with the detergent solution.

3 Blot until the liquid is absorbed.

4 Repeat Steps 2 and 3 until the stain disappears or is no longer absorbed into the cloth.

5 If the stain remains, use an eyedropper to apply hydrogen peroxide, and then apply a drop or two of ammonia (caution, see page 33).

6 Sponge with cold water and blot dry.

CARPET

1 Mix one tablespoon of liquid hand dishwashing detergent and one tablespoon of white vinegar with two cups of warm water.

2 Using a clean white cloth, sponge the stain with the detergent-vinegar solution.

3 Blot until the liquid is absorbed.

4 Repeat Steps 2 and 3 until the stain disappears or is no longer absorbed into the cloth.

5 If the stain remains, use an eyedropper to apply hydrogen peroxide, and then apply a drop or two of ammonia (caution, see page 33).

6 Sponge with cold water and blot dry.

BLEACH

FABRIC

1 Mix one tablespoon of sodium thiosulfate with one cup of warm water.

2 Using a clean white cloth, sponge the stain with the sodium thiosulfate solution.

3 Blot until the liquid is absorbed.

4 Repeat Steps 2 and 3 until the stain disappears.

5 Launder.

UPHOLSTERY

1 Mix one tablespoon of liquid hand dishwashing detergent with two cups of cool water.

2 Using a clean white cloth, sponge the stain with the detergent solution.

3 Blot until the liquid is absorbed.

4 Repeat Steps 2 and 3 until the stain disappears or is no longer absorbed into the cloth.

5 If the stain remains, mix one tablespoon of white vinegar with two cups of cool water. Sponge the stain with the solution. Blot until the liquid is absorbed.

6 Sponge with cold water and blot dry.

--- Worth a Try ---

You might be able to reclaim a mistakenly bleached item by dyeing it a darker color. Treat the item first with a color remover. This will help minimize the contrast between the bleach spots and the original color, increasing your chances that the item will dye evenly.

CARPET

1. Mix one tablespoon of liquid hand dishwashing detergent with two cups of warm water.
2. Using a clean white cloth, sponge the stain with the detergent solution.
3. Blot until the liquid is absorbed.
4. Repeat Steps 2 and 3 until the stain disappears or is no longer absorbed into the cloth.
5. If the stain remains, mix one tablespoon of white vinegar with two cups of warm water. Sponge the stain with the solution. Blot until the liquid is absorbed.
6. Sponge with cold water and blot dry.

HIDE THE SPOTS

If the bleach spots on your carpet or upholstery are small, you may be able to camouflage them. Look for a felt-tip fabric-marking pen (available in craft stores) that closely matches the original color. Check the ink color on a clean white cloth before applying it to your carpet or upholstery.

BLOOD

FABRIC

1. If the stain is fresh, soak in cold water or use an eyedropper to apply hydrogen peroxide directly to the stain. For dried stains, brush the stain well to remove the surface deposit, then pretreat or soak in cool water with a laundry product containing enzymes.
2. Launder.
3. If the stain remains, rewash using the recommended bleach.

UPHOLSTERY

1   Mix one tablespoon of liquid hand dishwashing detergent with two cups of cold water. If the stain has dried, brush it well to remove the surface deposit.

2   Using a clean white cloth, sponge the stain with the detergent solution.

3   Blot until the liquid is absorbed.

4   Repeat Steps 2 and 3 until the stain disappears.

5   Sponge with cold water and blot dry.

CARPET

1   Mix one tablespoon of liquid hand dishwashing detergent with two cups of cold water. If the stain has dried, brush it well to remove the surface deposit.

2   Using a clean white cloth, sponge the stain with the detergent solution.

3   Blot until the liquid is absorbed.

4   Repeat Steps 2 and 3 until the stain disappears or is no longer absorbed into the cloth.

5   If the stain remains, mix one tablespoon of ammonia (caution, see page 33) with $\frac{1}{2}$ cup of warm water.

6   Sponge the stain with the ammonia solution.

7   Blot until the liquid is absorbed.

8   Sponge with cold water and blot dry.

DISAPPEARING BLOOD STAINS

If you prick your finger while sewing and get blood stains on your project, immediately moisten an unbloodied finger with a bit of your own saliva and apply it to the stain. Watch it vanish!

FABRIC

1 Flush stain with cool water.
2 Mix one tablespoon of white vinegar and $1/2$ teaspoon of liquid laundry detergent with one quart of cool water.
3 Soak the stain in the vinegar-detergent solution for 15 minutes.
4 Rinse with cool water.
5 If the stain remains, sponge with rubbing alcohol and rinse thoroughly.
6 Launder, using chlorine bleach, if safe for the fabric.

UPHOLSTERY

1 Mix one tablespoon of white vinegar with $2/3$ cup of rubbing alcohol.
2 Sponge the stain with a clean white cloth and the vinegar-alcohol solution.
3 Blot until the liquid is absorbed.
4 Repeat Steps 2 and 3 until the stain disappears.
5 Sponge with cold water and blot dry.

CARPET

1 Mix one tablespoon of liquid hand dishwashing detergent with two cups of warm water.

2 Using a clean white cloth, sponge the stain with the detergent solution.

3 Blot until the liquid is absorbed.

4 Repeat Steps 2 and 3 until the stain disappears or is no longer absorbed into the cloth.

5 If the stain remains, mix one tablespoon of ammonia (caution, see page 33) with two cups of cold water.

6 Sponge the stain with the ammonia solution.

7 Blot until the liquid is absorbed.

8 Sponge with cold water and blot dry.

BLUSH

FABRIC

1 Pretreat with a prewash stain remover.

2 Launder.

UPHOLSTERY

method 1

1 Sponge the stain with a clean white cloth and dry-cleaning solvent.

2 Blot until the solvent is absorbed.

3 Repeat Steps 1 and 2 until the stain disappears.

method 2

1   Mix one tablespoon of liquid hand dishwashing detergent with two cups of cool water.

2   Sponge the stain with a clean white cloth and the detergent solution.

3   Blot until the liquid is absorbed.

4   Repeat Steps 2 and 3 until the stain disappears.

5   Sponge with cold water and blot dry.

....

CARPET

1   Sponge the stain with a clean white cloth and dry-cleaning solvent..

2   Blot until the solvent is absorbed.

3   Mix one tablespoon of liquid hand dishwashing detergent with two cups of warm water.

4   Sponge the stain with the detergent solution.

5   Blot until the liquid is absorbed.

6   Repeat Steps 4 and 5 until the stain disappears or is no longer absorbed into the cloth.

7   If the stain remains, mix one tablespoon of ammonia (caution, see page 33) with $1/2$ cup of water.

8   Sponge the stain with the ammonia solution.

9   Blot until the liquid is absorbed.

10 Repeat Steps 8 and 9 until the stain disappears or is no longer absorbed into the cloth.

11 If the stain remains, mix one tablespoon of white vinegar with two cups of warm water. Sponge the stain with the solution. Blot until the liquid is absorbed.

12 Sponge with cold water and blot dry.

TREATING MYSTERY STAINS

When all your attempts to identify a stain have failed (see "The Stain with No Name," page 50), try the following steps, in order, until the stain disappears. Note that these recommendations are for washable fabrics only. For mystery stains on upholstery and carpets, consult a cleaning professional.

1 Begin by assuming that the stain is oil-based. Sponge the stain with a dry-cleaning solvent. Let it air-dry.

2 Gently rub waterless hand cleaner into the stain. Let it stand for about 15 minutes. Repeat this process again. Rinse well.

3 Soak the stain in cold water for at least 30 minutes.

4 Mix one tablespoon of liquid laundry detergent with one cup of water. Add a few drops of white vinegar. Sponge the stain with this solution. Rinse well.

5 Mix one tablespoon of liquid laundry detergent with one of cup of water. Add a few drops of ammonia (caution, see page 33). Sponge the stain with this solution. Rinse well.

6 Sponge the stain with rubbing alcohol. Let it air-dry.

7 Rub liquid laundry detergent into the stained area. Let it stand for five minutes. Rinse well.

8 Soak the stain in an enzyme laundry product for at least 30 minutes, but no more than overnight. Launder.

9 The last solution for an unknown stain is to resort to bleach. Just be sure the stains are not caused by rust. The chemical reaction of rust to bleach will set the stains permanently.

And if all of this fails, air-dry the item and take it to a dry cleaner. Just be sure to let the cleaner know the steps you already have taken to remove the stain.

BROCCOLI

FABRIC

1 Scrape off excess broccoli.
2 Flush under cold running water to loosen the stain.
3 Pretreat with a prewash stain remover.
4 Launder, using the hottest water and type of bleach safe for the fabric.

UPHOLSTERY

1 Scrape off excess broccoli.
2 Mix one tablespoon of liquid hand dishwashing detergent with two cups of cool water.
3 Using a clean white cloth, sponge the stain with the detergent solution.
4 Blot until the liquid is absorbed.
5 Repeat Steps 3 and 4 until the stain disappears.
6 Sponge with cold water and blot dry.

CARPET

1 Scrape off excess broccoli.
2 Mix one tablespoon of liquid hand dishwashing detergent with two cups of warm water.
3 Using a clean white cloth, sponge the stain with the detergent solution.
4 Blot until the liquid is absorbed.
5 Repeat Steps 3 and 4 until the stain disappears.
6 Sponge with cold water and blot dry.

BUTTER

FABRIC

1 Scrape off excess butter.
2 Pretreat with a prewash stain remover.
3 Launder, using the hottest water safe for the fabric.

UPHOLSTERY

1 Scrape off excess butter.
2 Sprinkle baking soda, cornstarch, or other absorbent on the stain. Let stand 10 to 15 minutes, and then vacuum.
3 Using a clean white cloth, sponge the stain with a dry-cleaning solvent.
4 Blot until the solvent is absorbed.
5 Repeat Steps 3 and 4 until the stain disappears.

CARPET

1 Scrape off excess butter.
2 Sprinkle baking soda, cornstarch, or other absorbent on the stain. Let stand 10 to 15 minutes, and then vacuum.
3 Using a clean white cloth, sponge the stain with a dry-cleaning solvent.
4 Blot until the solvent is absorbed.
5 Repeat Steps 3 and 4 until the stain disappears or is no longer absorbed into the cloth.
6 If the stain remains, mix one tablespoon of liquid hand dishwashing detergent and one tablespoon of white vinegar with two cups of warm water.
7 Sponge the stain with the detergent-vinegar solution.
8 Blot until the liquid is absorbed.
9 Sponge with cold water and blot dry.

CANDLE WAX

FABRIC

1 If the wax is still soft, freeze the item to harden the wax, and then scrape off the excess wax.

2 Sponge with a dry-cleaning solvent.

3 Place the stain between clean paper towels and press with a warm iron to transfer the wax to the paper towels. Replace the paper towels frequently to absorb more wax and prevent the stain from transferring to other places on the fabric.

4 Pretreat with a prewash stain remover.

5 Launder, using chlorine bleach, if safe for the fabric, or oxygen bleach.

6 If any color remains, rewash.

UPHOLSTERY

1 If the wax is still soft, freeze it by applying an ice cube wrapped in a small plastic bag, and then scrape off the excess wax.

2 Using a clean white cloth, sponge the stain with a dry-cleaning solvent.

3 Blot until the solvent is absorbed.

4 Repeat Steps 2 and 3 until the stain disappears.

CARPET

1 If the wax is still soft, freeze it by applying an ice cube wrapped in a small plastic bag, and then scrape off the excess wax.

2 Sponge with a dry-cleaning solvent.

3 Cover the stain with a clean white cloth and press, using the tip of a warm iron to transfer the wax to the cloth. Repeat, using a clean portion of the cloth, until all the wax is transferred from the carpet to the cloth.

4 If a color stain remains, sponge the stain again with a dry-cleaning solvent.

5 Blot dry.

CARROT

FABRIC

1 Scrape off excess carrot.

2 Flush under cold running water to loosen the stain.

3 Pretreat with a prewash stain remover.

4 Launder, using the hottest water and the type of bleach that are safe for the fabric.

UPHOLSTERY

1 Scrape off excess carrot.

2 Mix one tablespoon of liquid hand dishwashing detergent with two cups of cool water.

3 Using a clean white cloth, sponge the stain with the detergent solution.

4 Blot until the liquid is absorbed.

5 Repeat Steps 3 and 4 until the stain disappears.

6 Sponge with cold water and blot dry.

CARPET

1 Scrape off excess carrot.

2 Mix one tablespoon of liquid hand dishwashing detergent with two cups of warm water.

3 Using a clean white cloth, sponge the stain with the detergent solution.

4 Blot until the liquid is absorbed.

5 Repeat Steps 3 and 4 until the stain disappears.

6 Sponge with cold water and blot dry.

CATSUP

FABRIC

1 Working from the back of the stain, flush with cold water.

2 Pretreat with a liquid laundry detergent, tamp the stain, and let stand for several minutes.

3 Rinse well.

4 Sponge with white vinegar.

5 Rinse well.

6 Repeat Steps 2 through 5 until you have removed as much of the stain as possible.

7 Pretreat with a prewash stain remover, and then launder.

8 If the stain remains, rub with a liquid laundry detergent, and then soak in warm water for up to 30 minutes.

9 Launder again, with bleach, if necessary.

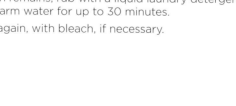

UPHOLSTERY

1 Sponge with cool water.
2 Mix one tablespoon of liquid hand dishwashing detergent with two cups of cool water.
3 Using a clean white cloth, sponge the stain with the detergent solution.
4 Blot until the liquid is absorbed.
5 Repeat Steps 3 and 4 until the stain disappears.
6 Sponge with cold water and blot dry.

CARPET

1 Sponge with cool water.
2 Mix one tablespoon of liquid hand dishwashing detergent with two cups of warm water.
3 Using a clean white cloth, sponge the stain with the detergent solution.
4 Blot until the liquid is absorbed.
5 Repeat Steps 3 and 4 until the stain disappears or is no longer absorbed into the cloth.
6 If the stain remains, mix one table-spoon of ammonia (caution, see page 33) with $1/2$ cup of warm water.
7 Sponge the stain with the ammonia solution.
8 Blot until the liquid is absorbed.
9 Sponge with cold water and blot dry.

CHALK

FABRIC

1 Pretreat with a prewash stain remover.
2 Launder, using the warmest water and type of bleach safe for the fabric.
3 If the stain remains, sponge with rubbing alcohol and launder again.

UPHOLSTERY

method 1

1 Sponge the stain with a clean white cloth and dry-cleaning solvent.
2 Blot until the solvent is absorbed.
3 Repeat Steps 1 and 2 until the stain disappears.

method 2

1 Mix one tablespoon of liquid hand dishwashing detergent with two cups of cool water.
2 Using a clean white cloth, sponge the stain with the detergent solution.
3 Blot until the liquid is absorbed.
4 Repeat Steps 2 and 3 until the stain disappears.
5 Sponge with cold water and blot dry.

CARPET

1 Vacuum up as much as possible.
2 Mix one tablespoon of liquid hand dishwashing detergent with two cups of warm water.
3 Using a clean white cloth, sponge the stain with the detergent solution.
4 Blot until the liquid is absorbed.
5 Repeat Steps 3 and 4 until the stain disappears.
6 Sponge with cold water and blot dry.

CHARCOAL

FABRIC

1 Pretreat with a prewash stain remover.
2 Launder, using the warmest water and type of bleach safe for the fabric.
3 If the stain remains, sponge with rubbing alcohol and launder again.

UPHOLSTERY

method 1

1 Sponge the stain with a clean white cloth and dry-cleaning solvent.
2 Blot until the solvent is absorbed.
3 Repeat Steps 1 and 2 until the stain disappears.

method 2

1 Mix one tablespoon of liquid hand dishwashing detergent with two cups of cool water.
2 Sponge the stain with a clean white cloth and detergent solution.
3 Blot until the liquid is absorbed.
4 Repeat Steps 2 and 3 until the stain disappears.
5 Sponge with cold water and blot dry.

CARPET

method 1

1 Sprinkle baking soda, cornstarch, or other absorbent on the stain. Let stand at least one hour, and then vacuum.
2 Using a clean white cloth, sponge the stain with a dry-cleaning solvent.
3 Blot until the solvent is absorbed.
4 Repeat Steps 2 and 3 until the stain disappears.

method 2

1 Mix one tablespoon of liquid hand dishwashing detergent with two cups of warm water.

2 Using a clean white cloth, sponge the stain with the detergent solution.

3 Blot until the liquid is absorbed.

4 Repeat Steps 2 and 3 until the stain disappears.

5 Sponge with cold water and blot dry.

CHEESE

FABRIC

1 Pretreat or soak, using a laundry product containing enzymes. Soak new stains for at least 30 minutes and older stains for several hours.

2 Launder.

UPHOLSTERY

method 1

1 Using a clean white cloth, sponge the stain with a dry-cleaning solvent.

2 Blot until the solvent is absorbed.

3 Repeat Steps 1 and 2 until the stain disappears.

method 2

1 Mix one tablespoon of liquid hand dishwashing detergent with two cups of cool water.

2 Using a clean white cloth, sponge the stain with the detergent solution.

3 Blot until the liquid is absorbed.

4 Repeat Steps 2 and 3 until the stain disappears.

5 Sponge with cold water and blot dry.

CARPET

1 Mix one tablespoon of liquid hand dishwashing detergent with two cups of warm water.

2 Using a clean white cloth, sponge the stain with the detergent solution.

3 Blot until the liquid is absorbed.

4 Repeat Steps 3 and 4 until the stain disappears or is no longer absorbed into the cloth.

5 If the stain remains, mix one tablespoon of ammonia (caution, see page 33) with two cups of warm water.

6 Sponge the stain with the ammonia solution.

7 Blot until the liquid is absorbed.

8 Sponge with cold water and blot dry.

CHEWING GUM

FABRIC

1 If the gum is still soft, freeze the item to harden the gum; scrape off excess gum.

2 Sponge with a dry-cleaning solvent.

3 Pretreat with a prewash stain remover.

4 Launder.

UPHOLSTERY

1 If the gum is still soft, freeze it by directly applying an ice cube; scrape off excess gum.

2 Using a clean white cloth, sponge the stain with a dry-cleaning solvent.

3 Blot until the solvent is absorbed.

4 Repeat Steps 2 and 3 until the stain disappears.

─── Worth a Try ───

In a pinch, rubbing white vinegar (full strength) into the gum may soften it enough that you can pry it away from the fabric.

CARPET

1 If the gum is still soft, freeze it by directly applying an ice cube; scrape off excess gum.

2 Using a clean white cloth, sponge the stain with a dry-cleaning solvent.

3 Blot until the solvent is absorbed.

4 Repeat Steps 2 and 3 until the stain disappears or is no longer absorbed into the cloth.

5 If the stain remains, mix one tablespoon of liquid hand dishwashing detergent and one tablespoon of white vinegar with two cups of warm water.

6 Sponge the stain with the detergent-vinegar solution.

7 Blot until the liquid is absorbed.

8 Sponge with cold water and blot dry.

ICE AND GUM

If you're using an ice cube to freeze the gum, don't wrap the ice in plastic food wrap. If you do, the plastic may stick to the gum, leaving you with an even bigger mess! You can, however, put it in a plastic sandwich bag, which is thicker and will not stick to the gum.

CHOCOLATE

FABRIC

1 Scrape off excess chocolate.
2 Pretreat with a prewash stain remover.
3 Launder.
4 If the stain remains, launder again, using the type of bleach that's safe for the fabric.

UPHOLSTERY

method 1

1 Scrape off excess chocolate.
2 Mix one tablespoon of liquid hand dishwashing detergent with two cups of cool water.
3 Using a clean white cloth, sponge the stain with the detergent solution.
4 Blot until the liquid is absorbed.
5 Repeat Steps 3 and 4 until the stain disappears.
6 Sponge with cold water and blot dry.

method 2

1 Using a clean white cloth, sponge the stain with a dry-cleaning solvent.
2 Blot until the solvent is absorbed.
3 Repeat Steps 1 and 2 until the stain disappears.

......

CARPET

1 Scrape off excess chocolate.
2 Mix one tablespoon of liquid hand dishwashing detergent with two cups of warm water.
3 Using a clean white cloth, sponge the stain with the detergent solution.
4 Blot until the liquid is absorbed.
5 Repeat Steps 3 and 4 until the stain disappears or is no longer absorbed into the cloth.
6 If the stain remains, mix one tablespoon of ammonia (caution, see page 33) with two cups of warm water.
7 Sponge the stain with the ammonia solution.
8 Blot until the liquid is absorbed.
9 Sponge with cold water and blot dry.

COCOA/HOT CHOCOLATE

FABRIC

1 Pretreat with a prewash stain remover.
2 Launder.
3 If the stain remains, launder again, using the type of bleach safe for the fabric.

UPHOLSTERY

method 1

1 Mix one tablespoon of liquid hand dishwashing detergent with two cups of cool water.

2 Using a clean white cloth, sponge the stain with the detergent solution.

3 Blot until the liquid is absorbed.

4 Repeat Steps 2 and 3 until the stain disappears.

5 Sponge with cold water and blot dry.

method 2

1 Using a clean white cloth, sponge the stain with a dry-cleaning solvent.

2 Blot until the solvent is absorbed.

3 Repeat Steps 1 and 2 until the stain disappears.

CARPET

1 Mix one tablespoon of liquid hand dishwashing detergent with two cups of warm water.

2 Using a clean white cloth, sponge the stain with the detergent solution.

3 Blot until the liquid is absorbed.

4 Repeat Steps 2 and 3 until the stain disappears or is no longer absorbed into the cloth.

5 If the stain remains, mix one tablespoon of ammonia (caution, see page 33) with two cups of warm water.

6 Sponge the stain with the ammonia solution.

7 Blot until the liquid is absorbed.

8 Sponge with cold water and blot dry.

COCONUT/JUICE

FABRIC

1 Scrape off or blot up excess coconut.
2 Flush under cold running water to loosen the stain.
3 Pretreat with a prewash stain remover.
4 Launder, using the hottest water and type of bleach safe for the fabric.

UPHOLSTERY

1 Scrape off or blot up excess coconut.
2 Mix one tablespoon of liquid hand dishwashing detergent with two cups of cool water.
3 Sponge the stain with a clean white cloth and the detergent solution.
4 Blot until the liquid is absorbed.
5 Repeat Steps 3 and 4 until the stain disappears.
6 Sponge with cold water and blot dry.

CARPET

1 Scrape off or blot up excess coconut.
2 Mix one tablespoon of liquid hand dishwashing detergent with two cups of warm water.
3 Sponge the stain with a clean white cloth and the detergent solution.
4 Blot until the liquid is absorbed.
5 Repeat Steps 3 and 4 until the stain disappears or is no longer absorbed into the cloth.
6 If the stain remains, mix one tablespoon of ammonia (caution, see page 33) with two cups of warm water.
7 Sponge the stain with the ammonia solution.
8 Blot until the liquid is absorbed.
9 Sponge with cold water and blot dry.

COFFEE

FABRIC

1 Sponge the stain with cool water or soak the item for about 30 minutes in cool water.
2 Pretreat with a prewash stain remover.
3 Launder. If it's safe for the fabric, add chlorine bleach to the wash.

....

UPHOLSTERY

method 1

1 Mix one tablespoon of liquid hand dishwashing detergent with two cups of cool water.
2 Using a clean white cloth, sponge the stain with the detergent solution.
3 Blot until the liquid is absorbed.
4 Repeat Steps 2 and 3 until the stain disappears.
5 Sponge with cold water and blot dry.

method 2

1 Using a clean white cloth, sponge the stain with a dry-cleaning solvent.
2 Blot until the solvent is absorbed.
3 Repeat Steps 1 and 2 until the stain disappears.

COFFEE AND CREAM

If there's cream (or milk) in the coffee that caused the stain, be sure to use an enzyme laundry detergent when washing the stained item.

Recommended by
THE GOOD HOUSEKEEPING RESEARCH INSTITUTE

Wine Away is a commercial stain remover that is effective for red wine, grape juice, pet accidents, coffee, and grease. Treat the stain with Wine Away, following the application instructions on the bottle.

CARPET

1 Blot up as much of the spilled coffee as possible.
2 Use plain water or mix one tablespoon of liquid hand dishwashing detergent and one tablespoon of white vinegar with two cups of warm water.
3 Using a clean white cloth, sponge the stain with plain water or the detergent-vinegar solution. Apply a little bit at a time, blotting frequently with a dry cloth until the stain disappears.
4 If using a detergent-vinegar solution, sponge with cold water and blot dry to remove the solution.

CONCEALER

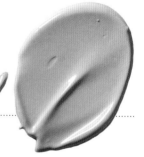

FABRIC

1 Pretreat with a prewash stain remover.
2 Launder.

UPHOLSTERY

method 1

1 Using a clean white cloth, sponge the stain with a dry-cleaning solvent.
2 Blot until the solvent is absorbed.
3 Repeat Steps 1 and 2 until the stain disappears.

method 2

1 Mix one tablespoon of liquid hand dishwashing detergent with two cups of cool water.

2 Using a clean white cloth, sponge the stain with the detergent solution.

3 Blot until the liquid is absorbed.

4 Repeat Steps 2 and 3 until the stain disappears.

5 Sponge with cold water and blot dry.

....

CARPET

1 Using a clean white cloth, sponge the stain with a dry-cleaning solvent.

2 Blot until the solvent is absorbed.

3 Mix one tablespoon of liquid hand dishwashing detergent with two cups of warm water.

4 Sponge the stain with the detergent solution.

5 Blot until the liquid is absorbed.

6 Repeat Steps 4 and 5 until the stain disappears or is no longer absorbed into the cloth.

7 If the stain remains, mix one tablespoon of ammonia (caution, see page 33) with $1/2$ cup of warm water.

8 Sponge the stain with the ammonia solution.

9 Blot until the liquid is absorbed.

10 Repeat Steps 8 and 9 until the stain disappears or is no longer absorbed into the cloth.

11 If the stain remains, mix one tablespoon of white vinegar with two cups of warm water. Sponge the stain with this solution. Blot until the liquid is absorbed.

12 Sponge with cold water and blot dry.

COOKING OIL

FABRIC

1 Blot up excess oil.
2 Pretreat with a prewash stain remover.
3 Launder, using the hottest water safe for the fabric.

UPHOLSTERY

1 Blot up excess oil.
2 Using a clean white cloth, sponge the stain with a dry-cleaning solvent.
3 Blot until the solvent is absorbed.
4 Repeat Steps 2 and 3 until the stain disappears.

CARPET

1 Blot up excess oil.
2 Sprinkle baking soda, cornstarch, or other absorbent on the stain. Let stand 10 to 15 minutes, and then vacuum.
3 Using a clean white cloth, sponge the stain with a dry-cleaning solvent.
4 Blot until the solvent is absorbed.
5 Repeat Steps 3 and 4 until the stain disappears or is no longer absorbed into the cloth.
6 If the stain remains, mix one tablespoon of liquid hand dishwashing detergent and one tablespoon of white vinegar with two cups of warm water. Sponge the stain with this solution. Blot until the liquid is absorbed.
7 Sponge with cold water and blot dry.

No Water, No Stain

Rub waterless hand cleaner into an oil-based stain on a washable fabric to help break up the stain.

CORRECTION FLUID, WATER-BASED → see PAINT, LATEX

CORRECTION FLUID, PETROLEUM-BASED

If you do not know which type of correction fluid caused the stain—water-based or petroleum-based—check the product label or contact the manufacturer. Correction fluid can be very difficult to remove. For fine carpets or highly visible spots on upholstery, it's wiser to contact a professional cleaner than to go the do-it-yourself route.

FABRIC

1 Scrape off excess correction fluid.
2 Place fabric face down and sponge the back of the fabric with acetone (caution, see page 32).
3 Turn garment faceup and sponge again with acetone.
4 Rinse well.
5 Repeat Steps 2 through 4 until you have removed as much fluid as possible.
6 Pretreat with a prewash stain remover.
7 Launder.

Correction Fluid, Petroleum-based continued

DURABLE OR DELICATE

The technique used to remove correction fluid (previous page) is for durable fabrics only. For delicate fabrics such as rayon, silk, or wool, or fabrics that contain acetate or triacetate fibers, consult a dry cleaner.

UPHOLSTERY

1 Scrape off excess correction fluid.
2 Using a clean white cloth, sponge the stain with a dry-cleaning solvent.
3 Blot until the solvent is absorbed.
4 If the stain remains, call a professional upholstery cleaner.

CARPET

1 Scrape off excess correction fluid.
2 Using a clean white cloth, sponge the stain with a dry-cleaning solvent.
3 Blot until the solvent is absorbed.
4 If the stain remains, call a professional carpet cleaner.

COTTAGE CHEESE

FABRIC

1 Pretreat or soak, using an enzyme laundry product. Soak for at least 30 minutes for new stains or several hours for older stains.
2 Launder.

UPHOLSTERY
method 1
1 Using a clean white cloth, sponge the stain with a dry-cleaning solvent.
2 Blot until the solvent is absorbed.
3 Repeat Steps 1 and 2 until the stain disappears.

method 2
1 Mix one tablespoon of liquid hand dishwashing detergent with two cups of cool water.
2 Using a clean white cloth, sponge the stain with the detergent solution.
3 Blot until the liquid is absorbed.
4 Repeat Steps 2 and 3 until the stain disappears.
5 Sponge with cold water and blot dry.

CARPET
1 Mix one tablespoon of liquid hand dishwashing detergent with two cups of warm water.
2 Using a clean white cloth, sponge the stain with the detergent solution.
3 Blot until the liquid is absorbed.
4 Repeat Steps 3 and 4 until the stain disappears or is no longer absorbed into the cloth.
5 If the stain remains, mix one tablespoon of ammonia (caution, see page 33) with two cups of warm water.
6 Sponge the stain with the ammonia solution.
7 Blot until the liquid is absorbed.
8 Sponge with cold water and blot dry.

COUGH SYRUP

FABRIC

1 Rinse in warm water to dilute the stain.

2 Mix one tablespoon of liquid laundry detergent and one tablespoon of white vinegar with two cups of cool water.

3 Sponge the stain with the detergent-vinegar solution; tamp with a brush or spoon.

4 Flush with water.

5 Sponge with rubbing alcohol.

6 Pretreat with a prewash stain remover.

7 Launder, using chlorine bleach, if safe for the fabric.

UPHOLSTERY

1 Mix one tablespoon of liquid hand dishwashing detergent and one tablespoon of white vinegar with two cups of cool water.

2 Sponge the stain with the detergent-vinegar solution; tamp with a brush or spoon.

3 Sponge with water; blot until the liquid is absorbed.

4 Sponge with rubbing alcohol; blot until the stain disappears or is no longer absorbed into the cloth.

5 Sponge with cold water and blot dry to remove the rubbing alcohol.

6 If the stain remains, mix one teaspoon of oxygen or nonchlorine bleach with one tablespoon of water. Test in an inconspicuous spot to be sure the mixture is safe to use. Using an eyedropper, apply the bleach solution to the stain. Sponge immediately with water; blot until the liquid is absorbed.

7 Sponge again with the detergent-vinegar solution.

8 Sponge with cold water and blot dry.

CARPET

1 Mix one tablespoon of liquid hand dishwashing detergent and one tablespoon of white vinegar with two cups of warm water.

2 Sponge the stain with the detergent-vinegar solution; tamp with a brush or spoon.

3 Sponge with water; blot until the liquid is absorbed.

4 Sponge with rubbing alcohol; blot until the stain disappears or is no longer absorbed into the cloth.

5 Sponge with cold water and blot dry to remove the rubbing alcohol.

6 If the stain remains, mix one teaspoon of oxygen or nonchlorine bleach with one tablespoon of water. Using an eyedropper, apply the bleach solution to the stain. Sponge immediately with water; blot until the liquid is absorbed.

7 Sponge again with the detergent-vinegar solution.

8 Sponge with cold water and blot dry.

CRANBERRY/JUICE/SAUCE

FABRIC

1 Flush stain with cool water.

2 Mix one tablespoon of white vinegar and $1/2$ teaspoon of liquid laundry detergent with one quart of cool water. Soak in this solution for 15 minutes.

3 Rinse with water.

4 If the stain remains, sponge the stain with rubbing alcohol and rinse thoroughly.

5 Launder, using chlorine bleach, if safe for the fabric.

....

UPHOLSTERY

1   Mix one tablespoon of white vinegar with $^2/_3$ cup of rubbing alcohol.
2   Using a clean white cloth, sponge the stain with the vinegar-alcohol solution.
3   Blot until the liquid is absorbed.
4   Repeat Steps 2 and 3 until the stain disappears.
5   Sponge with cold water and blot dry.

....

CARPET

1   Mix one tablespoon of liquid hand dishwashing detergent with two cups of cool water.
2   Using a clean white cloth, sponge the stain with the detergent solution.
3   Blot until the liquid is absorbed.
4   Repeat Steps 2 and 3 until the stain disappears or is no longer absorbed into the cloth.
5   If the stain remains, mix one tablespoon of ammonia (caution, see page 33) with two cups of warm water.
6   Sponge the stain with the ammonia solution.
7   Blot until the liquid is absorbed.
8   Sponge with cold water and blot dry.

— One More Cranberry Idea —

Another trick for a fresh cranberry stain: Hold the fabric taut over a bowl, and pour boiling water over the stain from about a foot away. You'll need a partner, and be careful not to splash.

CRAYON

FABRIC

method 1

1 If the crayon is soft, freeze the fabric to harden the crayon, and then scrape off the excess.

2 Place the stain between clean paper towels and press with a warm iron to transfer the stain to the paper towels. Replace the paper towels frequently to absorb more crayon and prevent the stain from transferring to other places on the fabric.

3 Pretreat with a prewash stain remover. Blot and let dry.

4 Launder with bleach that's appropriate for the fabric. If any color remains, rewash the item using chlorine bleach, if safe for the fabric, or oxygen bleach.

method 2

1 Place the stain facedown on a pad of paper towels. Spray with WD-40 and let it stand for a few minutes. Turn the fabric over and spray again with WD-40.

2 Apply liquid hand dishwashing detergent and work it into the stain. Replace the paper towels underneath as they absorb the stain.

3 Launder with chlorine bleach (if safe for the fabric) or oxygen bleach and the hottest water safe for the fabric. Rinse in warm water.

....

UPHOLSTERY

method 1

1 If the crayon is soft, freeze it by applying an ice cube wrapped in a small plastic bag, and then scrape off the excess crayon.

2 Using a clean white cloth, sponge the stain with a dry-cleaning solvent.

3 Blot until the solvent is absorbed.

4 Repeat Steps 2 and 3 until the stain disappears.

method 2

1 If the crayon is soft, freeze it by applying an ice cube wrapped in a small plastic bag, and then scrape off the excess crayon.

2 Spray the stain with WD-40 and let it stand for a few minutes.

3 Tamp the stain. Wipe off residue with a paper towel.

4 Respray with WD-40, then apply liquid hand dishwashing detergent directly on the sprayed area.

5 Tamp again. Wipe off the residue with a paper towel.

6 Repeat Steps 2 through 5 until the stain disappears.

CRAYON CARE

If crayons are accidentally laundered with clothes, you may end up with a whole load of crayon stains. Rewash the clothes with hot water, detergent, and one cup of baking soda. If the color still remains, launder using chlorine bleach, if safe for the fabric. If chlorine bleach isn't an option, pretreat or soak with oxygen bleach or an enzyme laundry product, using the hottest water safe for the fabric. Soak for at least 30 minutes, and then launder.

REMOVING CRAYON FROM THE DRYER DRUM

If crayon stains invade your dryer, spray a soft cloth with WD-40 and wipe the drum. Wash spots with a damp, sudsy cloth and rinse with a damp cloth. To make sure the drum is clean, run a load of dry rags through a drying cycle.

CARPET

method 1

1 If the crayon is soft, freeze it by applying an ice cube wrapped in a small plastic bag, and then scrape off the excess crayon.

2 Cover the stain with a clean white cloth and press, using the tip of a warm iron. Repeat, using a clean portion of the cloth until all the wax is transferred from the carpet to the cloth.

3 If a color stain remains, sponge the stain with a dry-cleaning solvent.

method 2

1 If the crayon is soft, freeze it by applying an ice cube wrapped in a small plastic bag, and then scrape off the excess crayon.

2 Spray the stain with WD-40 and let it stand for a few minutes.

3 Tamp the stain. Wipe off residue with a paper towel.

4 Respray with WD-40, then apply liquid hand dishwashing detergent directly on the sprayed area.

5 Tamp again. Wipe off the residue with a paper towel.

6 Repeat Steps 2 to 5 until the stain disappears.

THE TOP TEN KID STAINS

Kids in the house? There are sure to be stains on their clothes. Fast treatment is best, but not always possible. Here are two ideas to help.
(1) If the treatment calls for a prewash stain remover, use the stick type. It can stay on the (unwashed) clothes for up to a week. (2) Toss the item in the washing machine as soon as possible with lots of water and some detergent or a laundry presoak product. Let it soak. If you're dealing with a colored item, try not to soak it longer than overnight, which could damage the color. Here are the top ten kid stains and how to treat them.

1 **Baby food** Presoak in cold water and liquid laundry detergent. Launder in warm water. If the stain remains, pretreat with a prewash stain remover. Launder again.

2 **Blood** If the stain is fresh, flush with cold water and then soak in cold water. If it's a dried stain, pretreat or soak in warm water with an enzyme laundry product. Launder. If any stain remains, rewash the item, using the type of bleach that's safe for the fabric or sponge with hydrogen peroxide. Rewash the item.

3 **Chewing gum** If the gum is still soft, rub with an ice cube to harden it. Scrape off as much as possible with a dull knife. Sponge with a dry-cleaning solvent, rinse, and launder as usual or pretreat with a prewash stain remover; launder as usual.

4 **Crayon** Place the stain between clean paper towels and press with a warm iron to transfer the stain to the paper towels. Replace the paper towels frequently to absorb more wax and prevent the stain from transferring to other places on the fabric. Pretreat with a prewash stain remover. Blot and let dry. Launder. If any of the crayon color remains, rewash using chlorine bleach, if safe for the fabric, or oxygen bleach. You can also treat the stains with WD-40, following the directions on page 101.

5 Fruit juice Flush under cold running water. If the stain is old, soak for about 10 minutes in cold water, and then pretreat with a prewash stain remover. Launder, using the warmest water and type of bleach safe for the fabric.

6 Grass Pretreat with a prewash stain remover (one that contains enzymes). Launder, using the hottest water safe for the fabric and chlorine bleach, if safe for the fabric.

7 Milk Pretreat or soak, using an enzyme laundry product. Soak for at least 30 minutes or several hours for older stains. Launder.

8 Mud Let the mud dry, and then brush off as much as possible. Pretreat with a prewash stain remover; launder as usual.

9 Peanut butter and jelly Scrape off as much excess as possible. Tackle the oil (peanut butter) stain first by pretreating with a pre-wash stain remover. Then launder in the hot-test water safe for the fabric. If any stain

remains, treat the sugar and dye (jelly) stain next. Mix one tablespoon of white vinegar and $1/2$ teaspoon of liquid laundry detergent with one quart of warm water. Soak in this solution for 15 minutes. Rinse. If the stain remains, sponge with rubbing alcohol and rinse thoroughly. Launder, using chlorine bleach, if safe for the fabric.

10 Urine Pretreat or soak in warm water with an enzyme laundry product. Launder, using chlorine bleach, if safe for the fabric, or oxygen bleach.

CREAM

FABRIC

1 Pretreat or soak, using an enzyme laundry product. Soak for at least 30 minutes for new stains or several hours for older stains.

2 Launder.

....

UPHOLSTERY

method 1

1 Using a clean white cloth, sponge the stain with a dry-cleaning solvent.

2 Blot until the liquid is absorbed.

3 Repeat Steps 1 and 2 until the stain disappears.

method 2

1 Mix one tablespoon of liquid hand dishwashing detergent with two cups of cool water.

2 Using a clean white cloth, sponge the stain with the detergent solution.

3 Blot until the liquid is absorbed.

4 Repeat Steps 2 and 3 until the stain disappears.

5 Sponge with cold water and blot dry.

CARPET

1 Mix one tablespoon of liquid hand dishwashing detergent with two cups of warm water.
2 Using a clean white cloth, sponge the stain with the detergent solution.
3 Blot until the liquid is absorbed.
4 Repeat Steps 2 and 3 until the stain disappears or is no longer absorbed into the cloth.
5 If the stain remains, mix one tablespoon of ammonia (caution, see page 33) with two cups of warm water.
6 Sponge the stain with the ammonia solution.
7 Blot until the liquid is absorbed.
8 Sponge with cold water and blot dry.

CURRY

FABRIC

method 1

1 Rub glycerin into the stain with your fingertips and let it sit for a few minutes.
2 Rinse with cool water.
3 Launder, using the hottest water and type of bleach (chlorine bleach preferred) safe for the fabric.

method 2

1 Pretreat with a prewash stain remover.
2 Launder, using chlorine bleach, if safe for the fabric, or oxygen bleach.
3 If the stain persists, soak in a solution of one part hydrogen peroxide to nine parts cold water for at least 30 minutes.
4 Rinse, and then launder again.

....

UPHOLSTERY

1 Mix one tablespoon of liquid hand dishwashing detergent and one tablespoon of white vinegar with two cups of cool water.

2 Using a clean white cloth, sponge the stain with the detergent-vinegar solution. Leave it on the stain for at least 30 minutes, blotting every five minutes with a clean white cloth and more solution.

3 Sponge with cool water; blot until the liquid is absorbed.

4 Sponge the stain with rubbing alcohol; blot to remove the stain.

5 Sponge with water; blot until the liquid is absorbed.

6 If the stain remains, mix one teaspoon of liquid hand dishwashing detergent and one tablespoon of ammonia (caution, see page 33) with two cups of cool water.

7 Sponge the stain with the detergent-ammonia solution. Leave it on the stain for at least 30 minutes, blotting every five minutes with a clean white cloth and more solution.

8 Sponge with cold water and blot dry.

....

CARPET

1 Mix one tablespoon of liquid hand dishwashing detergent and one tablespoon of white vinegar with two cups of warm water.

2 Using a clean white cloth, sponge the stain with the detergent-vinegar solution. Blot frequently with a dry cloth until the stain disappears.

3 Sponge with plain water; blot until the liquid is absorbed.

4 Sponge the stain with rubbing alcohol; blot to remove the stain.

5 Sponge with water; blot until the liquid is absorbed.

6 If the stain remains, mix one teaspoon of liquid hand dishwashing detergent and one tablespoon of ammonia (caution, see page 33) with two cups of warm water.

7 Sponge the stain with the detergent-ammonia solution. Leave it on the stain for at least 30 minutes, blotting every five minutes with a clean white cloth and more solution.

8 Sponge with cold water and blot dry.

DEODORANT

FABRIC

1 Check to see if the stain has changed the color of the fabric. If so, apply ammonia (caution, see page 33) to fresh stains; white vinegar to old ones. Rinse.

2 Pretreat with a prewash stain remover.

3 Launder using the hottest water that's safe for the fabric. Stubborn stains may also respond to oxygen bleach in the hottest water safe for the fabric.

......

UPHOLSTERY

1 Mix one teaspoon of liquid hand dishwashing detergent and one tablespoon of ammonia (caution, see page 33) with two cups of warm water.

2 Using a clean white cloth, sponge the stain with the detergent-ammonia solution.

3 Blot until the liquid is absorbed.

4 If the stain remains, mix one tablespoon of liquid hand dishwashing detergent and one tablespoon of white vinegar with two cups of warm water.

5 Sponge the stain with the detergent-vinegar solution.

6 Blot until the liquid is absorbed.

7 If the stain remains, sponge the stain with rubbing alcohol.

8 Blot until the liquid is absorbed.

9 Sponge with cold water and blot dry.

CARPET

1 Mix one teaspoon of liquid hand dishwashing detergent and one tablespoon of ammonia (caution, see page 33) with two cups of warm water.
2 Using a clean white cloth, sponge the stain with the detergent-ammonia solution.
3 Blot until the liquid is absorbed.
4 If the stain remains, mix one tablespoon of liquid hand dishwashing detergent and one tablespoon of white vinegar with two cups of warm water.
5 Sponge the stain with the detergent-vinegar solution.
6 Blot until the liquid is absorbed.
7 If the stain remains, sponge the stain with rubbing alcohol.
8 Blot until the liquid is absorbed.
9 Sponge with cold water and blot dry.

DIRT

FABRIC

1 Let dry, if wet.
2 Brush off as much as possible.
3 Pretreat with a prewash stain remover.
4 Launder.

UPHOLSTERY

1 Let dry, if wet.
2 Vacuum up as much as possible.
3 Mix one tablespoon of liquid hand dishwashing detergent with two cups of cool water.
4 Using a clean white cloth, sponge the stain with the detergent solution.

5 Blot until the liquid is absorbed.

6 Repeat Steps 4 and 5 until the stain disappears.

7 Sponge with cold water and blot dry.

....

CARPET

1 Let dry, if wet.

2 Vacuum up as much as possible.

3 Mix one tablespoon of liquid hand dishwashing detergent with two cups of warm water.

4 Using a clean white cloth, sponge the stain with the detergent solution.

5 Blot until the liquid is absorbed.

6 Repeat Steps 4 and 5 until the stain disappears.

7 Sponge with cold water and blot dry.

DYE, RED

Dye transfer occurs when colors run in the wash or during drying, or when an item that has been overdyed rubs against another.

WHITE FABRIC ONLY

1 If chlorine bleach is safe for the fabric, mix a solution of $1/4$ cup of chlorine bleach per gallon of cool water and soak for 30 minutes.

2 Rinse, and then launder.

Recommended by
THE GOOD HOUSEKEEPING RESEARCH INSTITUTE

Red Erase is a product formulated for removing red stains, especially "kid stains" caused by items that contain artificial red colorings. Treat the stain with Red Erase, following the application instructions on the bottle.

WHITE OR COLORFAST FABRIC

1 Mix four gallons of the hottest water safe for the fabric with one packet of Carbona Color Run Remover. Be sure the remover is fully dissolved. (This product works on color from one item that's stained another—not when something like stripes bleeds onto itself.)

2 Add the dye-stained item and soak, stirring occasionally, until unwanted color is removed.

3 Rinse thoroughly in warm water.

4 For stubborn dyes, repeat Steps 1 through 3.

5 Launder.

UPHOLSTERY

1 Mix one teaspoon of liquid hand dishwashing detergent and one tablespoon of ammonia (caution, see page 33) with two cups of cool water.

2 Using a clean white cloth, sponge the stain with the detergent-ammonia solution.

3 Blot until the liquid is absorbed.

4 Repeat Steps 2 and 3 until the stain disappears or is no longer absorbed into the cloth.

5 If the stain remains, mix one tablespoon of liquid hand dishwashing detergent and one tablespoon of white vinegar with two cups of cool water.

6 Sponge the stain with the detergent-vinegar solution.

7 Blot until the liquid is absorbed.

8 Repeat Steps 6 and 7 until the stain disappears or is no longer absorbed into the cloth.

9 Sponge the stain with rubbing alcohol.

10 Blot until the liquid is absorbed.

11 Sponge with cold water and blot dry.

CARPET

1 Mix one teaspoon of liquid hand dishwashing detergent and one tablespoon of ammonia (caution, see page 33) with two cups of warm water.

2 Using a clean white cloth, sponge the stain with the detergent-ammonia solution.

3 Blot until the liquid is absorbed.

4 Repeat Steps 2 and 3 until the stain disappears or is no longer absorbed into the cloth.

5 If the stain remains, mix one tablespoon of liquid hand dishwashing detergent and one tablespoon of white vinegar with two cups of warm water.

6 Sponge the stain with the detergent-vinegar solution.

7 Blot until the liquid is absorbed.

8 Sponge the stain with rubbing alcohol.

9 Blot until the liquid is absorbed.

10 Sponge with cold water and blot dry.

DYE, ALL COLORS EXCEPT RED

Dye transfer occurs when colors run in the wash or during drying, or when an item that has been overdyed rubs against another.

WHITE FABRIC ONLY

1 If chlorine bleach is safe for the fabric, mix a solution of $1/4$ cup of chlorine bleach per gallon of cool water and soak for 30 minutes.

2 Rinse, and then launder.

WHITE OR COLORFAST FABRIC

1 Mix four gallons of the hottest water safe for the fabric with one packet of Carbona Color Run Remover. Be sure the remover is fully dissolved.

2 Add the dye-stained item and soak, stirring occasionally, until unwanted color is removed.

3 Rinse thoroughly in warm water.

4 For stubborn dyes, repeat Steps 1 through 3.

5 Launder.

UPHOLSTERY

1 Mix one tablespoon of liquid hand dishwashing detergent and one tablespoon of white vinegar with two cups of cool water.

2 Using a clean white cloth, sponge the stain with the detergent-vinegar solution. Leave it on the stain for at least 30 minutes, blotting every five minutes with a clean white cloth and more solution.

3 Sponge with cool water.

4 Blot until the liquid is absorbed.

5 Sponge the stain with rubbing alcohol; blot to remove the stain.

6 Sponge with alcohol; let the stain air-dry.

7 Sponge with cold water; blot until the liquid is absorbed.

8   If the stain remains, mix one teaspoon of liquid hand dishwashing detergent and one tablespoon of ammonia (caution, see page 33) with two cups of cool water.

9   Sponge the stain with the detergent-ammonia solution. Leave it on the stain for at least 30 minutes, blotting every five minutes with a clean white cloth and more solution.

10 Sponge with cold water and blot dry.

CARPET

1   Mix one tablespoon of liquid hand dishwashing detergent and one tablespoon of white vinegar with two cups of warm water.

2   Sponge the stain with a clean white cloth and the detergent-vinegar solution, blotting with a dry cloth until the stain disappears.

3   Flush with clear water.

4   Blot until the liquid is absorbed.

5   Sponge the stain with rubbing alcohol; blot to remove the stain.

6   Sponge with alcohol; let the stain air-dry.

7   Sponge with cold water; blot until the liquid is absorbed.

8   If the stain remains, mix one teaspoon of liquid hand dishwashing detergent and one tablespoon of ammonia (caution, see page 33) with two cups of warm water.

9   Sponge the stain with the detergent-ammonia solution. Leave it on the stain for at least 30 minutes, blotting every five minutes with a clean white cloth and more solution.

10 Sponge with cold water and blot dry.

JEANS: WASH FIRST

When it comes to transferring dye to other items, new denim jeans are a major offender. Pay attention to those tags that say "Wash before Wearing." They're there for a reason.

EGG

FABRIC

1 Scrape off excess egg.
2 Treat the stain with a prewash stain remover containing enzymes or soak for at least 30 minutes using an enzyme laundry detergent.
3 Launder.
4 If the stain remains, let the item air-dry, and then treat again with a prewash stain remover.
5 Launder, using hot water and chlorine bleach, if safe for the fabric.

UPHOLSTERY

1 Scrape off excess egg.
2 Mix one tablespoon of liquid hand dishwashing detergent with two cups of cool water.
3 Using a clean white cloth, sponge the stain with the detergent solution.
4 Blot until the liquid is absorbed.
5 Repeat Steps 3 and 4 until the stain disappears.
6 Sponge with cold water and blot dry.

CARPET

1 Scrape off excess egg.
2 Mix one tablespoon of liquid hand dishwashing detergent with two cups of warm water.
3 Using a clean white cloth, sponge the stain with the detergent solution.
4 Blot until the liquid is absorbed.
5 Repeat Steps 3 and 4 until the stain disappears or is no longer absorbed into the cloth.
6 If the stain remains, mix one tablespoon of ammonia (caution, see page 33) with two cups of warm water.
7 Sponge the stain with the ammonia solution.
8 Blot until the liquid is absorbed.
9 Sponge with cold water and blot dry.

EYE LINER

FABRIC

1 Pretreat with a prewash stain remover.
2 Launder.

UPHOLSTERY

method 1

1 Using a clean white cloth, sponge the stain with a dry-cleaning solvent.
2 Blot until the solvent is absorbed.
3 Continue applying and blotting the dry-cleaning solvent until the stain disappears.

method 2

1 Mix one tablespoon of liquid hand dishwashing detergent with two cups of cool water.

2 Using a clean white cloth, sponge the stain with the detergent solution.

3 Blot until the liquid is absorbed.

4 Repeat Steps 2 and 3 until the stain disappears.

5 Sponge with cold water and blot dry.

....

CARPET

1 Using a clean white cloth, sponge the stain with a dry-cleaning solvent.

2 Blot until the solvent is absorbed.

3 Mix one tablespoon of liquid hand dishwashing detergent with two cups of warm water.

4 Sponge the stain with the detergent solution.

5 Blot until the liquid is absorbed.

6 Repeat Steps 4 and 5 until the stain disappears or is no longer absorbed into the cloth.

7 If the stain remains, mix one tablespoon of ammonia (caution, see page 33) with $1/2$ cup of warm water.

8 Sponge the stain with the ammonia solution.

9 Blot until the liquid is absorbed.

10 Repeat Steps 8 and 9 until the stain disappears or is no longer absorbed into the cloth.

11 If the stain remains, mix one teaspoon of white vinegar with one cup of warm water. Sponge the stain with this solution. Blot until the liquid is absorbed.

12 Sponge with cold water and blot dry.

EYE SHADOW

FABRIC

1 Pretreat with a prewash stain remover.

2 Launder.

UPHOLSTERY

method 1

1 Using a clean white cloth, sponge the stain with a dry-cleaning solvent.

2 Blot until the solvent is absorbed.

3 Continue applying and blotting the dry-cleaning solvent until the stain disappears.

method 2

1 Mix one tablespoon of liquid hand dishwashing detergent with two cups of cool water.

2 Using a clean white cloth, sponge the stain with the detergent solution.

3 Blot until the liquid is absorbed.

4 Continue applying and blotting the detergent solution until the stain disappears.

5 Sponge with cold water and blot dry.

CARPET

1 Using a clean white cloth, sponge the stain with a dry-cleaning solvent.

2 Blot until the solvent is absorbed.

3 If the stain remains, mix one tablespoon of liquid hand dishwashing detergent with two cups of warm water.

4 Sponge the stain with the detergent solution.

5 Blot until the liquid is absorbed.

6 Mix one tablespoon of ammonia (caution, see page 33) with $1/2$ cup of warm water.

7 Sponge the stain with the ammonia solution.

8 Blot until the liquid is absorbed.

9 If the stain remains, mix one teaspoon of white vinegar with one cup of warm water. Sponge with this solution. Blot until the liquid is absorbed.

10 Sponge with cold water and blot dry.

FABRIC SOFTENER

FABRIC

1 Dampen the stain and rub with a bar of bath soap.

2 Launder.

SOFTENER AND STAINS

If you pour fabric softener directly onto your sheets, towels, clothes, or other items, blue-gray, greasy-looking stains may appear. To prevent this from happening, follow the directions on the fabric softener's label.

FECES

FABRIC

1 Pretreat or soak in warm water with a laundry product containing enzymes.

2 Launder, using chlorine bleach, if safe for the fabric, or oxygen bleach.

UPHOLSTERY

1 Mix one tablespoon of liquid hand dishwashing detergent with two cups of cool water.

2 Using a clean white cloth, sponge the stain with the detergent solution.

3 Blot until the liquid is absorbed.

4 Repeat Steps 2 and 3 until the stain disappears or is no longer absorbed into the cloth.

5 If the stain remains, use an eyedropper to apply hydrogen peroxide, and then apply a drop or two of ammonia (caution, see page 33).

6 Sponge with cold water and blot dry.

CARPET

1 Mix one tablespoon of liquid hand dishwashing detergent and one tablespoon of white vinegar with two cups of warm water.

2 Using a clean white cloth, sponge the stain with the detergent-vinegar solution.

3 Blot until the liquid is absorbed.

4 Repeat Steps 2 and 3 until the stain disappers or is no longer absorbed into the cloth.

5 If the stain remains, use an eyedropper to apply hydrogen peroxide, and then apply a drop or two of ammonia (caution, see page 33).

6 Sponge with cold water and blot dry.

FELT-TIP MARKER

FABRIC

1 Place the stain facedown on clean paper towels.

2 Sponge rubbing alcohol into the area around the stain, and then apply it directly to the stain.

3 Continue sponging the stain with alcohol, frequently changing the paper towels underneath, transferring as much ink as possible to the paper towels.

4 Rinse thoroughly.

5 Launder.

UPHOLSTERY

1 Mix one tablespoon of liquid hand dishwashing detergent and one tablespoon of white vinegar with two cups of cool water.

2 Using a clean white cloth, sponge the stain with the detergent-vinegar solution. Leave it on the stain for at least 30 minutes, blotting every five minutes with a clean white cloth and more solution.

3 Flush with cool water.

4 Blot until the liquid is absorbed.

5 Sponge the stain with rubbing alcohol. Blot to remove the stain.

6 Sponge with cold water.

7 Blot until the liquid is absorbed.

8 If the stain remains, mix one teaspoon of liquid hand dishwashing detergent and one tablespoon of ammonia (caution, see page 33) with two cups of cool water. Sponge the stain with this solution. Leave it on the stain for at least 30 minutes, blotting every five minutes with a clean white cloth and more solution.

9 Sponge with cold water and blot dry.

CARPET

1 Mix one tablespoon of liquid hand dishwashing detergent and one tablespoon of white vinegar with two cups of warm water.

2 Using a clean white cloth, sponge the stain with the detergent-vinegar solution, blotting frequently with a dry cloth until the stain disappears.

3 Flush with clear water.

4 Blot until the liquid is absorbed.

5 If the stain remains, sponge the stain with rubbing alcohol. Blot to remove the stain.

6 Flush with alcohol; let it air-dry.

7 Sponge with cold water.

8 Blot until the liquid is absorbed.

9 Mix one teaspoon of liquid hand dishwashing detergent and one tablespoon of ammonia (caution, see page 33) with two cups of warm water. Sponge the stain with this solution. Leave it on the stain for at least 30 minutes, blotting every five minutes with a clean white cloth and more solution.

10 Sponge with cold water and blot dry.

LAUNDERING THE LAUNDRY PEN

About 30 years ago, permanent markers were commonly known as "laundry pens," as they were often used for labeling clothing for school, camp, and so on. Today's laundry detergents are generally powerful enough to remove this ink from fabric, although it may take several washings and intensive treatment.

FOOD COLORING, RED

FABRIC

1   If the stain is fresh, sponge with cool water.

2   If the stain remains, mix a solution of $\frac{1}{4}$ cup of chlorine bleach, if safe for the fabric, or $\frac{1}{4}$ cup of oxygen bleach per gallon of cool water and soak for at least 30 minutes.

3   Rinse, and then launder.

UPHOLSTERY

1   Mix one teaspoon of liquid hand dishwashing detergent and one tablespoon of ammonia (caution, see page 33) with two cups of cool water.

2   Using a clean white cloth, sponge the stain with the detergent-ammonia solution.

3   Blot until the liquid is absorbed.

4   Repeat Steps 2 and 3 until the stain disappears or is no longer absorbed into the cloth.

5   If the stain remains, mix one tablespoon of liquid hand dishwashing detergent and one tablespoon of white vinegar with two cups of cool water.

6   Sponge the stain with the detergent-vinegar solution.

7   Blot until the liquid is absorbed.

8   Sponge the stain with rubbing alcohol.

9   Blot until the liquid is absorbed.

10 Sponge with cold water and blot dry.

CARPET

1 Mix one teaspoon of liquid hand dishwashing detergent and one tablespoon of ammonia (caution, see page 33) with two cups of warm water.

2 Using a clean white cloth, sponge the stain with the detergent-ammonia solution.

3 Blot until the liquid is absorbed.

4 Repeat Steps 2 and 3 until the stain disappears or is no longer absorbed into the cloth.

5 If the stain remains, mix one tablespoon of liquid hand dishwashing detergent and one tablespoon of white vinegar with two cups of warm water.

6 Sponge the stain with the detergent-vinegar solution.

7 Blot until the liquid is absorbed.

8 Sponge the stain with rubbing alcohol.

9 Blot until the liquid is absorbed.

10 Sponge with cold water and blot dry.

FOOD COLORING, ALL COLORS EXCEPT RED

FABRIC

1 If the stain is fresh, sponge with cool water.

2 Pretreat with a prewash stain remover.

3 Launder.

4 If the stain remains, mix a solution of $1/4$ cup of chlorine bleach, if safe for the fabric, or $1/4$ cup of oxygen bleach per gallon of cool water and soak for 30 minutes.

5 Rinse, and then launder.

UPHOLSTERY

1 Mix one tablespoon of liquid hand dishwashing detergent and one tablespoon of white vinegar with two cups of cool water.

2 Using a clean white cloth, sponge the stain with the detergent-vinegar solution. Leave it on the stain for at least 30 minutes, blotting every five minutes with a clean white cloth and more solution.

3 Sponge with cool water.

4 Blot until the liquid is absorbed.

5 Sponge with rubbing alcohol. Blot to remove the stain.

6 Sponge with cold water.

7 Blot until the liquid is absorbed.

8 If the stain remains, mix one teaspoon of liquid hand dishwashing detergent and one tablespoon of ammonia (caution, see page 33) with two cups of warm water. Sponge the stain with this solution. Leave it on the stain for at least 30 minutes, blotting every five minutes with a clean white cloth and more solution.

9 Sponge with cold water and blot dry.

CARPET

1 Mix one tablespoon of liquid hand dishwashing detergent and one tablespoon of white vinegar with two cups of warm water.

2 Using a clean white cloth, sponge the stain with the detergent-vinegar solution, blotting frequently with a dry cloth until the stain disappears.

3 Sponge with warm water and blot until the liquid is absorbed.

4 Sponge with rubbing alcohol. Blot to remove the stain.

5 Sponge with warm water and blot until the liquid is absorbed.

6 If the stain remains, mix one teaspoon of liquid hand dishwashing detergent and one tablespoon of ammonia (caution, see page 33) with two cups of warm water. Sponge the stain with this solution. Leave it on the stain for at least 30 minutes, blotting every five minutes with a clean white cloth and more solution.

7 Sponge with cold water and blot dry.

FORMULA

FABRIC

1 Pretreat with a prewash stain remover containing enzymes or soak for at least 30 minutes in a solution using an enzyme laundry detergent.

2 Launder.

3 If the stain remains, let the item air-dry, and then treat again with a prewash stain remover.

4 Launder, using hot water and chlorine bleach, if safe for the fabric.

UPHOLSTERY

1 Mix one tablespoon of liquid hand dishwashing detergent with two cups of cool water.
2 Using a clean white cloth, sponge the stain with the detergent solution.
3 Blot until the liquid is absorbed.
4 Repeat Steps 2 and 3 until the stain disappears.
5 Sponge with cold water and blot dry.

CARPET

1 Mix one tablespoon of liquid hand dishwashing detergent with two cups of warm water.
2 Using a clean white cloth, sponge the stain with the detergent solution.
3 Blot until the liquid is absorbed.
4 Repeat Steps 2 and 3 until the stain disappears or is no longer absorbed into the cloth.
5 If the stain remains, mix one tablespoon of ammonia (caution, see page 33) with two cups of warm water.
6 Sponge the stain with the ammonia solution.
7 Blot until the liquid is absorbed.
8 Sponge with cold water and blot dry.

— Baby Stains —

Treat baby-formula stains promptly. If left to set, they will become permanent.

FRUIT

See specific type of fruit (for example, apple) for instructions. For fruits not listed, follow these directions.

FABRIC

1 Scrape off excess fruit.
2 Flush under cold running water.
3 Launder, using the warmest water and type of bleach safe for the fabric.

. . . .

UPHOLSTERY

1 Scrape off excess fruit.
2 Mix one tablespoon of liquid hand dishwashing detergent with two cups of cold water.
3 Sponge the stain with a clean white cloth and the detergent solution.
4 Blot until the liquid is absorbed.
5 Repeat Steps 3 and 4 until the stain disappears.
6 Sponge with cold water and blot dry.

CARPET

1 Scrape off excess fruit.

2 Mix one tablespoon of liquid hand dishwashing detergent with two cups of cold water.

3 Using a clean white cloth, sponge the stain with the detergent solution.

4 Blot until the liquid is absorbed.

5 Repeat Steps 3 and 4 until the stain disappears or is no longer absorbed into the cloth.

6 If the stain remains, mix one tablespoon of ammonia (caution, see page 33) with two cups of cold water.

7 Sponge the stain with the ammonia solution.

8 Blot until the liquid is absorbed.

9 Sponge with cold water and blot dry.

FRUIT PUNCH

FABRIC

1 Pretreat with a heavy-duty laundry detergent.

2 Rinse thoroughly with cool water.

3 If the stain is still present, soak in a solution of $1/4$ cup of bleach (use chlorine bleach, if safe for the fabric) and one gallon of cool water. Soak for at least 30 minutes.

4 Launder.

UPHOLSTERY

1 Mix one tablespoon of liquid hand dishwashing detergent and one tablespoon of white vinegar with two cups of cool water.

2 Using a clean white cloth, sponge the stain with the detergent-vinegar solution. Leave it on the stain for at least 30 minutes, blotting every five minutes with a clean white cloth and more solution.

3 Sponge with cool water.

4 Blot until the liquid is absorbed.

5 Sponge the stain with rubbing alcohol. Blot to remove the stain.

6 Sponge with cold water.

7 If the stain remains, mix one teaspoon of liquid hand dishwashing detergent and one tablespoon of ammonia (caution, see page 33) with two cups of cool water. Sponge the stain with this solution. Leave it on the stain for at least 30 minutes, blotting every five minutes with a clean white cloth and more solution.

8 Sponge with cold water and blot dry.

CARPET

1 Mix one tablespoon of liquid hand dishwashing detergent and one tablespoon of white vinegar with two cups of warm water.

2 Using a clean white cloth, sponge the stain with the detergent-vinegar solution. Leave it on the stain for at least 30 minutes, blotting every five minutes with a clean white cloth and more solution.

3 Sponge with warm water.

4 Blot until the liquid is absorbed.

5 Sponge the stain with rubbing alcohol. Blot to remove the stain.

6 Sponge with cold water.

7 If the stain remains, mix one teaspoon of liquid hand dishwashing detergent and one tablespoon of ammonia (caution, see page 33) with two cups of warm water. Sponge the stain with this solution. Leave it on the stain for at least 30 minutes, blotting every five minutes with a clean white cloth and more solution.

8 Sponge with cold water and blot dry.

HAUNTING HALLOWEEN STAINS

Here are the most common Halloween stains on fabric and how to treat them.

APPLE JUICE Flush under cold running water. Launder, using the warmest water and type of bleach safe for the fabric.

CHEWING GUM If the gum is still soft, rub it with an ice cube to harden it. Then scrape off as much as possible with a dull knife. Pretreat with a prewash stain remover; launder as usual.

CHOCOLATE Pretreat with a prewash stain remover. Launder. If the stain remains, launder again, using the type of bleach safe for the fabric.

HAIR DYE If you are using a temporary hair dye, treat the stain with a prewash stain remover and then launder in the hottest water that's safe for the fabric. If you are using a permanent hair dye, determine if chlorine bleach is safe for the fabric. If it is, mix a solution of $1/4$ cup of chlorine bleach per gallon of cool water and soak for 30 minutes. Rinse, and then launder. If chlorine bleach isn't safe for the fabric, mix one cup of ammonia (caution, see page 33) with one gallon of warm water. Hold the fabric taut over a jar or bucket and pour the ammonia mixture directly onto the stain, allowing it to drain through the fabric. Rinse, and then launder.

HAIR GEL Pretreat with a prewash stain remover and then launder with the hottest water that's safe for the fabric.

MAKEUP Pretreat with a prewash stain remover. Launder.

NAIL POLISH Place the fabric facedown on a clean white cloth or paper towels and blot with acetone (caution, see page 32). Rinse with clear water. Repeat blotting with acetone and rinsing until the stain no longer transfers to the cloth or paper towels. Apply a prewash stain remover. Launder.
Beware! Many purchased Halloween costumes are made from fabrics that contain acetate fibers. Unfortunately, acetone, which removes nail polish, also melts acetate fibers. The nail polish will disappear, but you'll be left with a hole in the fabric. Check the label to make sure the fabric doesn't contain acetate. No label? Put a little bit of acetone on a cotton swab and rub it onto an inconspicuous place on the garment. If it creates a small hole, you'll know the fabric contains acetate.

PUMPKIN PULP Scrape off the excess. Flush under cold running water. Launder, using the warmest water and type of bleach safe for the fabric.

FURNITURE POLISH

FABRIC

1 Pretreat with a prewash stain remover.
2 Launder.
3 If any stain remains, rewash using chlorine bleach, if safe for the fabric, or oxygen bleach.

UPHOLSTERY

1 Using a clean white cloth, sponge the stain with a dry-cleaning solvent.
2 Blot until the solvent is absorbed.
3 Repeat Steps 1 and 2 until the stain disappears.

CARPET

1 Using a clean white cloth, sponge the stain with a dry-cleaning solvent.
2 Blot until the solvent is absorbed.
3 Repeat Steps 1 and 2 until the stain disappears or is no longer absorbed into the cloth.
4 If the stain remains, mix one tablespoon of liquid hand dishwashing detergent and one tablespoon of white vinegar with two cups of warm water.
5 Sponge the stain with the detergent-vinegar solution.
6 Blot until the liquid is absorbed.
7 Sponge with cold water and blot dry.

FURNITURE-POLISH CULPRIT

Furniture polish contains cleaning agents, but it's the oil in most formulas that will leave a stain on fabric, upholstery, and carpet.

GASOLINE

FABRIC

1 Sprinkle baking soda, cornstarch, or other absorbent on the stain. Let stand for about 30 minutes, and then brush off.

2 Pretreat with a prewash stain remover.

3 Launder, using the hottest water safe for the fabric. Let fabric air-dry until you are certain that the stain is completely removed. Do not use the clothes dryer.

UPHOLSTERY

1 Sprinkle baking soda, cornstarch, or other absorbent on the stain. Let stand for 10 to 15 minutes, and then vacuum.

2 Using a clean white cloth, sponge the stain with a dry-cleaning solvent.

3 Blot until the solvent is absorbed.

4 Repeat Steps 2 and 3 until the stain disappears.

CARPET

1 Sprinkle baking soda, cornstarch, or other absorbent on the stain. Let stand for 10 to 15 minutes, and then vacuum.

2 Using a clean white cloth, sponge the stain with a dry-cleaning solvent.

3 Blot until the solvent is absorbed.

4 If the stain remains, mix one tablespoon of liquid hand dishwashing detergent and one tablespoon of white vinegar with two cups of warm water. Sponge the stain with this solution. Blot until the liquid is absorbed.

5 Sponge with cold water and blot dry to remove the detergent-vinegar solution.

GLUE, WATER-BASED CRAFT

There are different types of glues on the market. If you are removing a glue that is not a water-based craft glue, contact the glue manufacturer for stain-removal recommendations.

FABRIC

1 Scrape off excess glue.
2 Pretreat with a prewash stain remover.
3 Launder, using the hottest water that's safe for the fabric.

UPHOLSTERY

1 Scrape off excess glue.
2 Mix one tablespoon of liquid hand dishwashing detergent with two cups of cool water.
3 Sponge the stain with a clean white cloth and the detergent solution.
4 Blot until the liquid is absorbed.
5 Repeat Steps 3 and 4 until the stain disappears.
6 Sponge with cold water and blot dry.

CARPET

1 Scrape off excess glue.
2 Mix one tablespoon of liquid hand dishwashing detergent with two cups of warm water.
3 Sponge the stain with a clean white cloth and the detergent solution.
4 Blot until the liquid is absorbed.
5 If the stain remains, mix one tablespoon of ammonia (caution, see page 33) with two cups of warm water.
6 Sponge the stain with the ammonia solution.
7 Blot until the liquid is absorbed.
8 Sponge with cold water and blot dry.

HARDENED GLUE

If the glue has hardened, you'll need to soften it before you can scrape it off. There are several ways to do this:

1 Rub petroleum jelly into the stain.

2 Rub waterless hand cleaner into the stain.

3 Fold several paper towels until you have a stack about $1/8$ inch thick. Saturate with warm water and then place the stack on top of the glue stain. Leave the paper towels in place for about an hour, until the glue softens.

GRAPE JUICE

FABRIC

1 Flush the stain with cool water.

2 Mix one tablespoon of white vinegar and $1/2$ teaspoon of liquid laundry detergent with one quart of warm water. Soak in this solution for 15 minutes.

3 Rinse with water.

4 If the stain remains, sponge with rubbing alcohol and rinse thoroughly.

5 Launder, using chlorine bleach, if safe for the fabric.

UPHOLSTERY

1 Mix one tablespoon of white vinegar with $2/3$ cup of rubbing alcohol.

2 Using a clean white cloth, sponge the stain with the vinegar-alcohol solution.

3 Blot until the liquid is absorbed.

4 Repeat Steps 2 and 3 until the stain disappears.

5 Sponge with cold water and blot dry.

Wine Away is a commercial stain remover that is effective for red wine, grape juice, pet accidents, coffee, and grease. Treat the stain with Wine Away, following the application instructions on the bottle.

CARPET

1 Mix one tablespoon of liquid hand dishwashing detergent with two cups of warm water.
2 Using a clean white cloth, sponge the stain with the detergent solution.
3 Blot until the liquid is absorbed.
4 Repeat Steps 2 and 3 until the stain disappears or is no longer absorbed into the cloth.
5 If the stain remains, mix one tablespoon of ammonia (caution, see page 33) with two cups of warm water.
6 Sponge the stain with the ammonia solution.
7 Blot until the liquid is absorbed.
8 Sponge with cold water and blot dry.

GRAPEFRUIT/JUICE

FABRIC

1 Flush the stain with cold running water.
2 Pretreat with a prewash stain remover.
3 Launder, using the hottest water and type of bleach safe for the fabric.

UPHOLSTERY

1 Mix one tablespoon of liquid hand dishwashing detergent with two cups of cool water.

2 Using a clean white cloth, sponge the stain with the detergent solution.

3 Blot until the liquid is absorbed.

4 Repeat Steps 2 and 3 until the stain disappears.

5 Sponge with cold water and blot dry.

CARPET

1 Mix one tablespoon of liquid hand dishwashing detergent with two cups of warm water.

2 Using a clean white cloth, sponge the stain with the detergent solution.

3 Blot until the liquid is absorbed.

4 Repeat Steps 2 and 3 until the stain disappears or is no longer absorbed into the cloth.

5 If the stain remains, mix one tablespoon of ammonia (caution, see page 33) with two cups of warm water.

6 Sponge the stain with the ammonia solution.

7 Blot until the liquid is absorbed.

8 Sponge with cold water and blot dry.

GRASS

FABRIC

1 Pretreat with a prewash stain remover or rub liquid laundry detergent with enzymes into the stain.

2 Launder, using the hottest water safe for the fabric and chlorine bleach, if safe for the fabric.

....

UPHOLSTERY

1 Using a clean white cloth, sponge the stain with acetone (caution, see page 32), if safe for the fabric.

2 Sponge the stain with a dry-cleaning solvent.

3 Blot until the solvent is absorbed.

4 If the stain remains, mix one tablespoon of liquid handwashing detergent with two cups of cool water.

5 Sponge the stain with the detergent solution.

6 Blot until the liquid is absorbed.

7 Mix one tablespoon of ammonia (caution, see page 33) with two cups of cool water.

8 Sponge the stain with the ammonia solution.

9 Blot until the liquid is absorbed.

10 Sponge with cold water and blot dry.

....

CARPET

1 Using a clean white cloth, sponge the stain with acetone (caution, see page 32).

2 Sponge the stain with a dry-cleaning solvent.

3 Blot until the solvent is absorbed.

4 If the stain remains, mix one tablespoon of liquid handwashing detergent with two cups of warm water.

5 Sponge the stain with the detergent solution.

6 Blot until the liquid is absorbed.

7 Mix one tablespoon of ammonia (caution, see page 33) with two cups of warm water.

8 Sponge the stain with the ammonia solution.

9 Blot until the liquid is absorbed.

10 Sponge with cold water and blot dry.

Grass stains are a mixture of green chlorophyll, protein, and other organic matter. Because chlorophyll tends to set into the fabric immediately, it makes grass stains so challenging to remove.

GRAVY

FABRIC

1 Scrape off excess gravy.
2 Pretreat with a prewash stain remover.
3 Launder, using the hottest water safe for the fabric.

UPHOLSTERY

1 Scrape off excess gravy.
2 Sprinkle baking soda, cornstarch, or other absorbent on the stain. Let stand 10 to 15 minutes, and then vacuum.
3 Sponge the stain with a clean white cloth and dry-cleaning solvent.
4 Blot until the solvent is absorbed.
5 Repeat Steps 3 and 4 until the stain disappears.

GRAVY MAGNETS

Ever notice how your finest table linens are magnets for gravy? Don't let this discourage you from using them. Once the celebration is over, treat any stains ASAP with a prewash stain remover. Then toss your linens in the washing machine along with an enzyme detergent and bleach. Let the linens agitate for a few minutes, then turn off the washing machine and soak the linens overnight. Finish the wash cycle in the morning. Check to be sure the stains are gone before putting the linens in the dryer.

....

CARPET

1   Scrape off excess gravy.

2   Sprinkle baking soda, cornstarch, or other absorbent on the stain. Let stand for 10 to 15 minutes, and then vacuum.

3   Using a clean white cloth, sponge the stain with a dry-cleaning solvent.

4   Blot until the solvent is absorbed.

5   Repeat Steps 3 and 4 until the stain disappears or is no longer absorbed into the cloth.

6   If the stain remains, mix one tablespoon of liquid hand dishwashing detergent and one tablespoon of white vinegar with two cups of warm water. Sponge the stain with this solution. Blot until the liquid is absorbed.

7   Sponge with cold water and blot dry to remove the detergent-vinegar solution.

GREASE

FABRIC

1   Pretreat with a prewash stain remover.

2   Launder, using the hottest water safe for the fabric.

....

UPHOLSTERY

1   Scrape off excess grease.

2   Sprinkle baking soda, cornstarch, or other absorbent on the stain. Let stand 10 to 15 minutes, and then vacuum.

3   Using a clean white cloth, sponge the stain with a dry-cleaning solvent.

4   Blot until the solvent is absorbed.

5   Repeat Steps 3 and 4 until the stain disappears.

Clean Hands, Clean Stains

Waterless hand cleaner can do more than just clean your hands. It's a great emergency spot treatment for oily, greasy stains on washable fabrics. Just rub it into the stain, then rinse or sponge the stain with cool water. Follow up with the recommended stain-removal procedure.

CARPET

1 Scrape off excess grease.
2 Sprinkle baking soda, cornstarch, or other absorbent on the stain. Let stand for 10 to 15 minutes, and then vacuum.
3 Using a clean white cloth, sponge the stain with a dry-cleaning solvent.
4 Blot until the solvent is absorbed.
5 If the stain remains, mix one tablespoon of liquid hand dishwashing detergent and one tablespoon of white vinegar with two cups of warm water. Sponge the stain with this solution. Blot until the liquid is absorbed.
6 Sponge with cold water and blot dry to remove the detergent-vinegar solution.

GUM → see CHEWING GUM

HAIR CONDITIONER

FABRIC

1 Pretreat with a prewash stain remover.
2 Launder, using the hottest water safe for the fabric.

UPHOLSTERY

1 Scrape off excess conditioner.
2 Sprinkle baking soda, cornstarch, or other absorbent on the stain. Let stand 10 to 15 minutes, and then vacuum.
3 Using a clean white cloth, sponge the stain with a dry-cleaning solvent.
4 Blot until the solvent is absorbed.
5 Repeat Steps 3 and 4 until the stain disappears.

CARPET

1 Scrape off excess conditioner.
2 Sprinkle baking soda, cornstarch, or other absorbent on the stain. Let stand for 10 to 15 minutes, and then vacuum.
3 Using a clean white cloth, sponge the stain with a dry-cleaning solvent.
4 Blot until the solvent is absorbed.
5 If the stain remains, mix one tablespoon of liquid hand dishwashing detergent and one tablespoon of white vinegar with two cups of warm water. Sponge the stain with this solution. Blot until the liquid is absorbed.
6 Sponge with cold water and blot dry to remove the detergent-vinegar solution.

HAIR DYE

FABRIC

method 1

1 If chlorine bleach is safe for the fabric, mix a solution of $1/4$ cup of chlorine bleach per gallon of cool water and soak for 30 minutes.

2 Rinse, and then launder.

method 2

1 If chlorine bleach isn't safe for the fabric, mix one cup of ammonia (caution, see page 33) with one gallon of cool water. Hold the fabric taut over a jar or bucket and pour the ammonia mixture directly onto the stain, allowing it to drain through the fabric.

2 Rinse, and then launder.

....

UPHOLSTERY

1 Mix one tablespoon of liquid hand dishwashing detergent and one tablespoon of white vinegar with two cups of cool water.

2 Using a clean white cloth, sponge the stain with the detergent-vinegar solution. Leave it on the stain for at least 30 minutes, blotting every five minutes with a clean white cloth and more solution.

3 Sponge with cold water.

4 Blot until the liquid is absorbed.

5 Sponge the stain with rubbing alcohol. Blot to remove the stain.

6 Sponge with cold water.

7 If the stain remains, mix one teaspoon of liquid hand dishwashing detergent and one tablespoon of ammonia (caution, see page 33) with two cups of cool water. Sponge the stain with this solution. Leave it on the stain for at least 30 minutes, blotting every five minutes with a clean white cloth and more solution.

8 Sponge with cold water and blot dry.

WORTH A TRY ON FABRIC

If you can't launder the hair-dye stain immediately, grab some hairspray and saturate the fabric. The alcohol in the hairspray helps loosen the stain. As soon as you can, soak and then launder the stain.

CARPET

1 Mix one tablespoon of liquid hand dishwashing detergent and one tablespoon of white vinegar with two cups of warm water.
2 Using a clean white cloth, sponge the stain with the detergent-vinegar solution, blotting frequently with a dry cloth until the stain disappears.
3 Sponge with cold water.
4 Blot until the liquid is absorbed.
5 Sponge the stain with rubbing alcohol. Blot to remove the stain.
6 Sponge with cold water.
7 If the stain remains, mix one teaspoon of liquid hand dishwashing detergent and one tablespoon of ammonia (caution, see page 33) with two cups of warm water. Sponge the stain with this solution. Leave it on the stain for at least 30 minutes, blotting every five minutes with a clean white cloth and more solution.
8 Sponge with cold water and blot dry.

WORTH A TRY ON CARPET OR UPHOLSTERY

If the hair-dye stain doesn't completely disappear on carpet or uphol-stery, use an eye dropper to apply hydrogen peroxide. (Test the hydrogen peroxide in a hidden spot for safety first.) Let dry for 24 hours, and then repeat, if necessary. If this treatment removes the original color of the carpet or upholstery along with the stain, try using a felt-tip fabric mark-ing pen (available in craft stores) as close as possible to the original color to fix the stained area. Check the ink color on a clean white cloth before applying it to your carpet or upholstery.

HAIR GEL

FABRIC

1 Scrape off excess gel.
2 Pretreat with a prewash stain remover.
3 Launder, using the hottest water safe for the fabric.

UPHOLSTERY

1 Scrape off excess gel.
2 Sprinkle baking soda, cornstarch, or other absorbent on the stain. Let stand 10 to 15 minutes, and then vacuum.
3 Using a clean white cloth, sponge the stain with a dry-cleaning solvent.
4 Blot until the solvent is absorbed.
5 Repeat Steps 3 and 4 until the stain disappears.

CARPET

1 Scrape off excess gel.
2 Sprinkle baking soda, cornstarch, or other absorbent on the stain. Let stand for 10 to 15 minutes, and then vacuum.
3 Using a clean white cloth, sponge the stain with a dry-cleaning solvent.
4 Blot until the solvent is absorbed.
5 If the stain remains, mix one tablespoon of liquid hand dishwashing detergent and one tablespoon of white vinegar with two cups of warm water. Sponge the stain with this solution. Blot until the liquid is absorbed.
6 Sponge with cold water and blot dry to remove the detergent-vinegar solution.

HAIRSPRAY

FABRIC

1 Pretreat with a prewash stain remover.

2 Launder.

UPHOLSTERY

method 1

1 Using a clean white cloth, sponge the stain with a dry-cleaning solvent.

2 Blot until the solvent is absorbed.

3 Repeat Steps 1 and 2 until the stain disappears.

method 2

1 Mix one tablespoon of liquid hand dishwashing detergent with two cups of cool water.

2 Using a clean white cloth, sponge the stain with the detergent solution.

3 Blot until the liquid is absorbed.

4 Repeat Steps 2 and 3 until the stain disappears.

5 Sponge with cold water and blot dry.

CARPET

1 Using a clean white cloth, sponge the stain with a dry-cleaning solvent.

2 Blot until the solvent is absorbed.

3 Mix one tablespoon of liquid hand dishwashing detergent with two cups of warm water.

4 Sponge the stain with the detergent solution.

5 Blot until the liquid is absorbed.

6 Mix one tablespoon of ammonia (caution, see page 33) with $1/2$ cup of water.

7 Sponge the stain with the ammonia solution.

8 Blot until the liquid is absorbed.

9 If the stain remains, mix one teaspoon of white vinegar with one cup of warm water. Sponge the stain with this solution. Blot until the liquid is absorbed.

10 Sponge with cold water and blot dry.

HONEY

FABRIC

1 Scrape off excess honey.

2 Flush under cold running water to loosen the stain.

3 Pretreat with a prewash stain remover.

4 Launder, using the hottest water and type of bleach safe for the fabric.

....

UPHOLSTERY

1 Scrape off excess honey.

2 Mix one tablespoon of liquid hand dishwashing detergent with two cups of cool water.

3 Using a clean white cloth, sponge the stain with the detergent solution.

4 Blot until the liquid is absorbed.

5 Repeat Steps 3 and 4 until the stain disappears.

6 Sponge with cold water and blot dry.

CARPET

1 Scrape off excess honey.
2 Mix one tablespoon of liquid hand dishwashing detergent with two cups of warm water.
3 Using a clean white cloth, sponge the stain with the detergent solution.
4 Blot until the liquid is absorbed.
5 Repeat Steps 3 and 4 until the stain disappears.
6 If the stain remains, mix one tablespoon of ammonia (caution, see page 33) with two cups of warm water.
7 Sponge the stain with the ammonia solution.
8 Blot until the liquid is absorbed.
9 Sponge with cold water and blot dry.

ICE CREAM

FABRIC

1 Pretreat or soak, using an enzyme laundry product. Soak for at least 30 minutes or several hours for older stains.
2 Launder.

UPHOLSTERY
method 1

1 Using a clean white cloth, sponge the stain with a dry-cleaning solvent.
2 Blot until the solvent is absorbed.
3 Repeat Steps 1 and 2 until the stain disappears.

method 2

1 Mix one tablespoon of liquid hand dishwashing detergent with two cups of cool water.
2 Using a clean white cloth, sponge the stain with the detergent solution.
3 Blot until the liquid is absorbed.
4 Repeat Steps 2 and 3 until the stain disappears.
5 Sponge with cold water and blot dry.

....

CARPET

1 Mix one tablespoon of liquid hand dishwashing detergent with two cups of warm water.
2 Using a clean white cloth, sponge the stain with the detergent solution.
3 Blot until the liquid is absorbed
4 Repeat Steps 2 and 3 until the stain disappears or is no longer absorbed into the cloth.
5 If the stain remains, mix one tablespoon of ammonia (caution, see page 33) with two cups of warm water.
6 Sponge the stain with the ammonia solution.
7 Blot until the liquid is absorbed.
8 Sponge with cold water and blot dry.

STAIN STICKS

Ice-cream stains have a way of occurring far from home. Keep a prewash stain stick in the picnic basket, backpack, diaper bag, glove compartment— any place that's handy. These sticks are specially formulated to put any stain "on hold" for up to a week.

INK, BALLPOINT

FABRIC

1 Sponge with a dry-cleaning solvent until the ink stops bleeding.
2 Rinse thoroughly.
3 Sponge the stain with rubbing alcohol. Let it air-dry.
4 If the stain remains, rub liquid laundry detergent into the stain. Let it stand overnight.
5 Rinse.
6 Apply prewash stain remover.
7 Launder.

UPHOLSTERY

1 Using a clean white cloth, sponge the stain with a dry-cleaning solvent.
2 Blot until the solvent is absorbed.
3 Repeat Steps 1 and 2 until the stain disappears.

CARPET

1 Using a clean white cloth, sponge the stain with a dry-cleaning solvent.
2 Blot until the solvent is absorbed.
3 Mix one tablespoon of liquid hand dishwashing detergent and one tablespoon of white vinegar with two cups of warm water.
4 Sponge the stain with the detergent-vinegar solution.
5 Blot until the liquid is absorbed.
6 Repeat Steps 1 through 5 until the stain disappears.
7 Sponge with cold water and blot dry to remove the detergent-vinegar solution.

IODINE

FABRIC

1 For fresh stains, flush with cold water.

2 Soak in a solution of one quart cool water, $1/2$ teaspoon of bleach-free liquid laundry detergent, and one tablespoon of ammonia (caution, see page 33) for about 30 minutes.

3 Launder.

4 For old or persistent stains, mix one tablespoon of sodium thiosulfate with one cup of cool water. Using a clean white cloth, sponge the stain with this solution. Rinse well.

5 Launder again.

UPHOLSTERY

1 Mix one tablespoon of liquid hand dishwashing detergent with two cups of cool water.

2 Using a clean white cloth, sponge the stain with the detergent solution. Let stand for about 30 minutes.

3 Blot until the liquid is absorbed.

4 Repeat Steps 2 and 3 until the stain disappears.

5 Sponge with cold water and blot dry to remove the detergent solution.

6 For stubborn stains, mix one tablespoon of sodium thiosulfate with one cup of cool water. Apply to the stained area with an eye dropper. Add a few drops of ammonia (caution, see page 33). Blot until the liquid is absorbed.

7 Sponge with cold water and blot dry.

Iodine & Bleach

Do not use a detergent that contains bleach on an iodine stain. Bleach can set iodine stains, making them more difficult to remove.

CARPET

1 Using a clean white cloth, sponge the stain with a dry-cleaning solvent.

2 Blot until the solvent is absorbed.

3 If the stain remains, mix one tablespoon of sodium thiosulfate with one cup of warm water. Sponge the stain with this solution. Blot until the liquid is absorbed.

4 Sponge with cold water and blot dry.

JAM

FABRIC

1 Flush the stain with cool water.

2 Mix one tablespoon of white vinegar and $1/2$ teaspoon of liquid laundry detergent with one quart of warm water. Soak in this solution for 15 minutes.

3 Rinse with water.

4 If the stain remains, sponge with rubbing alcohol and rinse thoroughly.

5 Launder, using chlorine bleach, if safe for the fabric.

UPHOLSTERY

1 Mix one tablespoon of white vinegar with $^2/_3$ cup of rubbing alcohol.

2 Using a clean white cloth, sponge the stain with the vinegar-alcohol solution.

3 Blot until the liquid is absorbed.

4 Repeat Steps 2 and 3 until the stain disappears.

5 Sponge with cold water and blot dry.

CARPET

1 Mix one tablespoon of liquid hand dishwashing detergent with two cups of warm water.

2 Using a clean white cloth, sponge the stain with the detergent solution.

3 Blot until the liquid is absorbed.

4 Repeat Steps 2 and 3 until the stain disappears or is no longer absorbed into the cloth.

5 If the stain remains, mix one tablespoon of ammonia (caution, see page 33) with two cups of warm water.

6 Sponge the stain with the ammonia solution.

7 Blot until the liquid is absorbed.

8 Sponge with cold water and blot dry.

JELLY

FABRIC

1 Flush stain with cool water.
2 Mix one tablespoon of white vinegar and $1/2$ teaspoon of liquid laundry detergent with one quart of warm water. Soak in this solution for 15 minutes.
3 Rinse with water.
4 If the stain remains, sponge with rubbing alcohol and rinse thoroughly.
5 Launder, using chlorine bleach, if safe for the fabric.

UPHOLSTERY

1 Mix one tablespoon of white vinegar with $2/3$ cup of rubbing alcohol.
2 Using a clean white cloth, sponge the stain with the vinegar-alcohol solution.
3 Blot until the liquid is absorbed.
4 Repeat Steps 2 and 3 until the stain disappears.
5 Sponge with cold water and blot dry.

CARPET

1 Mix one tablespoon of liquid hand dishwashing detergent with two cups of warm water.

2 Using a clean white cloth, sponge the stain with the detergent solution.

3 Blot until the liquid is absorbed.

4 Repeat Steps 2 and 3 until the stain disappears or is no longer absorbed into the cloth.

5 If the stain remains, mix one tablespoon of ammonia (caution, see page 33) with two cups of warm water.

6 Sponge the stain with the ammonia solution.

7 Blot until the liquid is absorbed.

8 Sponge with cold water and blot dry.

JUICE → see SPECIFIC TYPE OF JUICE (FOR EXAMPLE, APPLE JUICE)

THE DIFFERENCE BETWEEN JAM AND JELLY

Jam and jelly are both made from fruit mixed with sugar and pectin. Jam uses crushed fruit or fruit pulp, which is boiled, while jelly is created from juice. Jelly is usually easier to spread than jam. Both can create tough-to-remove stains if you don't get to them right away.

LEMON/JUICE

FABRIC

1 Flush the stain with cold running water.

2 Pretreat with a prewash stain remover.

3 Launder, using the hottest water and the type of bleach that are safe for the fabric.

UPHOLSTERY

1 Mix one tablespoon of liquid hand dishwashing detergent with two cups of cool water.

2 Using a clean white cloth, sponge the stain with the detergent solution.

3 Blot until the liquid is absorbed.

4 Repeat Steps 2 and 3 until the stain disappears.

5 Sponge with cold water and blot dry.

CARPET

1 Mix one tablespoon of liquid hand dishwashing detergent with two cups of warm water.

2 Using a clean white cloth, sponge the stain with the detergent solution.

3 Blot until the liquid is absorbed.

4 Repeat Steps 2 and 3 until the stain disappears or is no longer absorbed into the cloth.

5 If the stain remains, mix one tablespoon of ammonia (caution, see page 33) with two cups of warm water.

6 Sponge the stain with the ammonia solution.

7 Blot until the liquid is absorbed.

8 Sponge with cold water and blot dry.

LIGHTER FLUID

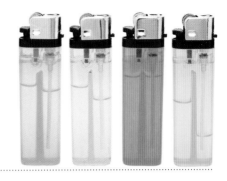

FABRIC

1 Pretreat with a prewash stain remover.
2 Launder.

UPHOLSTERY

1 Mix one tablespoon of liquid hand dishwashing detergent with two cups of cool water.
2 Using a clean white cloth, sponge the stain with the detergent solution.
3 Blot until the liquid is absorbed.
4 Repeat Steps 2 and 3 until the stain disappears.
5 Sponge with cold water and blot dry.

CARPET

1 Mix one tablespoon of liquid hand dishwashing detergent with two cups of warm water.
2 Using a clean white cloth, sponge the stain with the detergent solution.
3 Blot until the liquid is absorbed.
4 Repeat Steps 2 and 3 until the stain disappears.
5 Sponge with cold water and blot dry.

TYPES OF LIGHTER FLUID

Lighter fluid consists of butane (cigarette lighters), naphtha (a hydro-carbon mixture in wick lighters), and a petroleum solvent (charcoal lighter).

LIME/JUICE

FABRIC

1 Flush the stain under cold running water.
2 Pretreat with a prewash stain remover.
3 Launder, using the hottest water and type of bleach safe for the fabric.

UPHOLSTERY

1 Mix one tablespoon of liquid hand dishwashing detergent with two cups of cool water.
2 Using a clean white cloth, sponge the stain with the detergent solution.
3 Blot until the liquid is absorbed.
4 Repeat Steps 2 and 3 until the stain disappears.
5 Sponge with cold water and blot dry.

CARPET

1 Mix one tablespoon of liquid hand dishwashing detergent with two cups of warm water.
2 Using a clean white cloth, sponge the stain with the detergent solution.
3 Blot until the liquid is absorbed.
4 Repeat Steps 2 and 3 until the stain disappears or is no longer absorbed into the cloth.
5 If the stain remains, mix one tablespoon of ammonia (caution, see page 33) with two cups of warm water.
6 Sponge the stain with the ammonia solution.
7 Blot until the liquid is absorbed.
8 Sponge with cold water and blot dry.

LIP BALM

FABRIC

method 1

1 Scrape off excess lip balm.
2 Pretreat with a prewash stain remover.
3 Launder.
4 If the stain remains, treat again with prewash stain remover.

method 2

1 Scrape off excess lip balm.
2 Pretreat with a prewash stain remover.
3 Launder.
4 Using a clean, white cloth, apply a dry-cleaning solvent to the stained area. Blot until the liquid is absorbed. Repeat, applying and blotting the solution until the stain disappears.
5 Launder again.

UPHOLSTERY

1 Scrape off excess lip balm.
2 Using a clean white cloth, sponge the stain with a dry-cleaning solvent.
3 Blot until the solvent is absorbed.
4 Repeat Steps 2 and 3 until the stain disappears.

KEEP YOUR BALM COOL

The main ingredients in most lip balms, wax and/or petroleum, can cause a nasty stain if left to melt in a pocket or in the clothes dryer.

CARPET

1 Scrape off excess lip balm.

2 Using a clean white cloth, sponge the stain with a dry-cleaning solvent.

3 Blot until the solvent is absorbed.

4 Repeat Steps 2 and 3 until the stain disappears or is no longer absorbed into the cloth.

5 If the stain remains, mix one tablespoon of liquid hand dishwashing detergent and one tablespoon of white vinegar with two cups of warm water.

6 Sponge the stain with the detergent-vinegar solution.

7 Blot until the liquid is absorbed.

8 Sponge with cold water and blot dry.

LIPSTICK

FABRIC

method 1

1 Scrape off excess lipstick.

2 Pretreat with a prewash stain remover.

3 Launder.

4 If the stain remains, treat again with prewash stain remover.

method 2

1 Scrape off excess lipstick.

2 Pretreat with a prewash stain remover.

3 Launder.

4 Using a clean, white cloth, apply a dry-cleaning solvent to the stained area. Blot until the liquid is absorbed. Repeat, applying and blotting the solution until the stain disappears.

5 Launder again.

UPHOLSTERY

1 Scrape off excess lipstick.
2 Using a clean white cloth, sponge the stain with a dry-cleaning solvent.
3 Blot until the solvent is absorbed.
4 Repeat Steps 2 and 3 until the stain disappears.

CARPET

1 Scrape off excess lipstick.
2 Using a clean white cloth, sponge the stain with a dry-cleaning solvent.
3 Blot until the solvent is absorbed.
4 Repeat Steps 2 and 3 until the stain disappears or is no longer absorbed into the cloth.
5 If the stain remains, mix one tablespoon of liquid hand dishwashing detergent and one tablespoon of white vinegar with two cups of warm water.
6 Sponge the stain with the detergent-vinegar solution.
7 Blot until the liquid is absorbed.
8 Sponge with cold water and blot dry.

VALENTINE STAINS WE LOVE TO HATE

Here are the most common Valentine stains on fabric and how to treat them.

CANDLE WAX If the wax is still soft, freeze to harden, and then scrape off the excess. Sponge with a dry-cleaning fluid. Place the stain between clean paper towels and press with a warm iron to transfer the wax to the paper towels. Replace the paper towels frequently to absorb more wax and prevent the stain from transferring to other places on the fabric. Pretreat with a prewash stain remover. Launder. If any color remains, rewash using chlorine bleach, if safe for the fabric, or oxygen bleach.

CHAMPAGNE Sponge the spot with cool water or soak for about 30 minutes in a basin of cool water. Pretreat with a prewash stain remover. Launder. If it's safe for the fabric, add chlorine bleach to the wash.

CHOCOLATE Pretreat with a prewash stain remover. Launder. If the stain remains, launder again, using the type of bleach that's safe for the fabric.

COFFEE Sponge the spot with cool water or soak for about 30 minutes in a basin of cool water. Pretreat with a prewash stain remover. Launder. If it's safe for the fabric, add chlorine bleach to the wash.

FIREPLACE ASHES Hold the fabric taut and vacuum off as much soot as possible. Sprinkle an absorbent, such as talcum powder or baking soda, on the stain. Let it stand for several minutes, then vacuum again. Pretreat with a prewash stain remover or liquid laundry detergent. Launder.

LIPSTICK Scrape off excess lipstick. Pretreat with a pre-wash stain remover. Launder. If the stain remains, treat again with a prewash stain remover and then launder again, using chlorine bleach, if safe for the fabric. Alternatively, you can sponge with a dry-cleaning solvent, rinse, and then launder.

PERFUME Pretreat with a prewash stain remover. Launder.

POLLEN Gently shake the stained item to remove as much pollen as you can. Gently vacuum the fabric to remove more. Use the sticky side of a piece of tape to lift off the remaining particles. Pretreat with a prewash stain remover. Launder with fabric-appropriate bleach.

LOTION, HAND, FACIAL, OR BODY

FABRIC

1 Scrape off excess lotion.

2 Pretreat with a prewash stain remover.

3 Launder, using the hottest water safe for the fabric.

UPHOLSTERY

1 Scrape off excess lotion.

2 Sprinkle baking soda, cornstarch, or other absorbent on the stain. Let stand 10 to 15 minutes, and then vacuum.

3 Using a clean white cloth, sponge the stain with a dry-cleaning solvent.

4 Blot until the solvent is absorbed.

5 Repeat Steps 3 and 4 until the stain disappears.

CARPET

1 Scrape off excess lotion.

2 Sprinkle baking soda, cornstarch, or other absorbent on the stain. Let stand for 10 to 15 minutes, and then vacuum.

3 Using a clean white cloth, sponge the stain with a dry-cleaning solvent.

4 Blot until the solvent is absorbed.

5 Repeat Steps 3 and 4 until the stain disappears or is no longer absorbed into the cloth.

6 If the stain remains, mix one tablespoon of liquid hand dishwashing detergent and one tablespoon of white vinegar with two cups of warm water. Sponge the stain with this solution. Blot until the liquid is absorbed.

7 Sponge with cold water and blot dry.

MANGO

FABRIC

1 Scrape off excess mango.
2 Flush under cold running water.
3 Launder, using the warmest water
   and type of bleach safe for the fabric.

UPHOLSTERY

1 Scrape off excess mango.
2 Mix one tablespoon of liquid hand dishwashing detergent with
   two cups of cool water.
3 Using a clean white cloth, sponge the stain with the detergent
   solution.
4 Blot until the liquid is absorbed.
5 Repeat Steps 3 and 4 until the stain disappears.
6 Sponge with cold water and blot dry.

CARPET

1 Scrape off excess mango.
2 Mix one tablespoon of liquid hand dishwashing detergent with
   two cups of warm water.
3 Using a clean white cloth, sponge the stain with the detergent
   solution.
4 Blot until the liquid is absorbed.
5 Repeat Steps 3 and 4 until the stain disappears or is no longer
   absorbed into the cloth.
6 If the stain remains, mix one tablespoon of ammonia (caution, see
   page 33) with two cups of warm water.
7 Sponge the stain with the ammonia solution.
8 Blot until the liquid is absorbed.
9 Sponge with cold water and blot dry.

MAPLE SYRUP

FABRIC

1 Working from the back of the stain, flush with warm water.

2 Pretreat with a liquid laundry detergent; tamp the stain, and let stand for several minutes.

3 Rinse well.

4 Sponge with white vinegar.

5 Rinse well.

6 Repeat steps 2 through 5 until you have removed as much stain as possible.

7 Pretreat with a prewash stain remover, and then launder.

8 If the stain remains, rub with a liquid laundry detergent, and then soak in warm water for up to 30 minutes.

9 Launder.

UPHOLSTERY

1 Mix one tablespoon of liquid hand dishwashing detergent with two cups of cool water.

2 Using a clean white cloth, sponge the stain with the detergent solution.

3 Blot until the liquid is absorbed.

4 Repeat Steps 2 and 3 until the stain disappears.

5 Sponge with cold water and blot dry.

CARPET

1 Mix one tablespoon of liquid hand dishwashing detergent with two cups of warm water.

2 Using a clean white cloth, sponge the stain with the detergent solution.

3 Blot until the liquid is absorbed.

4 Repeat Steps 2 and 3 until the stain disappears or is no longer absorbed into the cloth.

5 If the stain remains, mix one tablespoon of ammonia (caution, see page 33) with $1/2$ cup of warm water.

6 Sponge the stain with the ammonia solution.

7 Blot until the liquid is absorbed.

8 Sponge with cold water and blot dry.

MARGARINE

FABRIC

1 Scrape off excess margarine.

2 Pretreat with a prewash stain remover.

3 Launder, using the hottest water safe for the fabric.

UPHOLSTERY

1 Scrape off excess margarine.

2 Sprinkle baking soda, cornstarch, or other absorbent on the stain. Let stand 10 to 15 minutes, and then vacuum.

3 Using a clean white cloth, sponge the stain with a dry-cleaning solvent.

4 Blot until the solvent is absorbed.

5 Repeat Steps 3 and 4 until the stain disappears.

CARPET

1 Scrape off excess margarine.
2 Sprinkle baking soda, cornstarch, or other absorbent on the stain. Let stand for 10 to 15 minutes, and then vacuum.
3 Using a clean white cloth, sponge the stain with a dry-cleaning solvent.
4 Blot until the solvent is absorbed.
5 If the stain remains, mix one tablespoon of liquid hand dishwashing detergent and one tablespoon of white vinegar with two cups of warm water. Sponge the stain with this solution. Blot until the liquid is absorbed.
6 Sponge with cold water and blot dry to remove the detergent-vinegar solution.

MASCARA

FABRIC

1 Pretreat with a prewash stain remover.
2 Launder.

UPHOLSTERY

method 1

1 Using a clean white cloth, sponge the stain with a dry-cleaning solvent.
2 Blot until the solvent is absorbed.
3 Repeat Steps 1 and 2 until the stain disappears.

method 2

1 Mix one tablespoon of liquid hand dishwashing detergent with two cups of cool water.

2 Using a clean white cloth, sponge the stain with the detergent solution.

3 Blot until the liquid is absorbed.

4 Repeat Steps 2 and 3 until the stain disappears.

5 Sponge with cold water and blot dry.

....

CARPET

1 Using a clean white cloth, sponge the stain with a dry-cleaning solvent.

2 Blot until the solvent is absorbed.

3 Repeat Steps 1 and 2 until the stain disappears or is no longer absorbed into the cloth.

4 If the stain remains, mix one tablespoon of liquid hand dishwashing detergent with two cups of warm water.

5 Sponge the stain with the detergent solution.

6 Blot until the liquid is absorbed.

7 Mix one tablespoon of ammonia (caution, see page 33) with $1/2$ cup of water.

8 Sponge the stain with the ammonia solution.

9 Blot until the liquid is absorbed.

10 If the stain remains, mix one teaspoon of white vinegar with one cup of warm water. Sponge the stain with this solution. Blot until the liquid is absorbed.

11 Sponge with cold water and blot dry.

CLEOPATRA'S MASCARA

Ancient Egyptian mascara blended kohl and honey with crocodile dung—sounds like a recipe for one terrible stain!

MAYONNAISE

FABRIC

1 Scrape off excess mayonnaise.
2 Pretreat with a prewash stain remover.
3 Launder, using the hottest water safe for the fabric.

UPHOLSTERY

1 Scrape off excess mayonnaise.
2 Sprinkle baking soda, cornstarch, or other absorbent on the stain. Let stand 10 to 15 minutes, and then vacuum.
3 Using a clean white cloth, sponge the stain with a dry-cleaning solvent.
4 Blot until the solvent is absorbed.
5 Repeat Steps 3 and 4 until the stain disappears.

CARPET

1 Scrape off excess mayonnaise.
2 Sprinkle baking soda, cornstarch, or other absorbent on the stain. Let stand 10 to 15 minutes, and then vacuum.
3 Using a clean white cloth, sponge the stain with a dry-cleaning solvent.
4 Blot until the solvent is absorbed.
5 If the stain remains, mix one tablespoon of liquid hand dishwashing detergent and one tablespoon of white vinegar with two cups of warm water. Sponge the stain with this solution. Blot until the liquid is absorbed.
6 Sponge with cold water and blot dry to remove the detergent-vinegar solution.

MEDICINE, ALCOHOL-BASED

FABRIC

1　Flush the stain with cold water.

2　Pretreat with an enzyme laundry product. Let stand for several minutes.

3　Rinse well with cold water.

4　Launder.

5　If the stain remains, pretreat with a liquid enzyme detergent. Soak in cold water for at least 30 minutes, agitating the fabric occasionally.

6　Launder, using the warmest water and type of bleach safe for the fabric.

....

UPHOLSTERY

method 1

1　Mix one tablespoon of white vinegar with ²/₃ cup of rubbing alcohol.

2　Using a clean white cloth, sponge the stain with the vinegar-alcohol solution.

3　Blot until the liquid is absorbed.

4　Repeat Steps 2 and 3 until the stain disappears.

method 2

1　Mix one tablespoon of liquid hand dishwashing detergent with two cups of cool water.

2　Using a clean white cloth, sponge the stain with the detergent solution.

3　Blot until the liquid is absorbed.

4　Repeat Steps 2 and 3 until the stain disappears.

5　Sponge with cold water and blot dry.

Recommended by
THE GOOD HOUSEKEEPING
RESEARCH INSTITUTE

LIMITED WARRANTY *to* CONSUMERS
· **GOOD** ·
HOUSEKEEPING
Since ★ 1909
REPLACEMENT *or* REFUND *if* DEFECTIVE

Red Erase is formulated for removing red stains, especially "kid stains" caused by items that contain artificial red colorings. Treat the stain with Red Erase, following the application instructions on the bottle.

CARPET

1 Using clean white paper towels or cloths, blot up as much of the medicine as possible.

2 Use plain water or mix one tablespoon of liquid hand dishwashing detergent and one tablespoon of white vinegar with two cups of warm water.

3 Using a clean white cloth, sponge the stain with a small amount of plain water or the detergent-vinegar solution. Apply a little at a time, blotting with a dry cloth until the stain disappears.

4 If using a detergent-vinegar solution, sponge with cold water and blot dry to remove the solution.

MEDICINE, OIL-BASED

FABRIC

1 Pretreat with a prewash stain remover.

2 Launder, using the hottest water safe for the fabric.

UPHOLSTERY

1 Scrape off excess medicine.

2 Sprinkle baking soda, cornstarch, or other absorbent on the stain. Let stand 10 to 15 minutes, and then vacuum.

3 Sponge the stain with a clean white cloth and dry-cleaning solvent.

4 Blot until the solvent is absorbed.

5 Repeat Steps 3 and 4 until the stain disappears.

CARPET

1 Scrape off excess medicine.

2 Sprinkle baking soda, cornstarch, or other absorbent on the stain. Let stand 10 to 15 minutes, and then vacuum.

3 Using a clean white cloth, sponge the stain with a dry-cleaning solvent.

4 Blot until the solvent is absorbed.

5 If the stain remains, mix one tablespoon of liquid hand dishwashing detergent and one tablespoon of white vinegar with two cups of warm water. Sponge the stain with this solution. Blot until the liquid is absorbed.

6 Sponge with cold water and blot dry to remove the detergent-vinegar solution.

CHEMICAL CULPRITS

Despite all your best efforts, some stains can't be removed because they contain chemicals that destroy or change the dye. One culprit is benzoyl peroxide, which can be found in acne medications, fade or age creams, and foot-care preparations. Another is dimethylsulfoxide, which is an ingredient in some arthritis medications. Before attempting to remove a stain, check the product label for the list of the medication's ingredients.

MELON

FABRIC

1 Scrape off excess melon.

2 Flush under cold running water.

3 Launder, using the warmest water and type of bleach safe for the fabric.

UPHOLSTERY

1 Scrape off excess melon.
2 Mix one tablespoon of liquid hand dishwashing detergent with two cups of cool water.
3 Using a clean white cloth, sponge the stain with the detergent solution.
4 Blot until the liquid is absorbed.
5 Repeat Steps 3 and 4 until the stain disappears.
6 Sponge with cold water and blot dry.

CARPET

1 Scrape off excess melon.
2 Mix one tablespoon of liquid hand dishwashing detergent with two cups of warm water.
3 Using a clean white cloth, sponge the stain with the detergent solution.
4 Blot until the liquid is absorbed.
5 Repeat Steps 3 and 4 until the stain disappears or is no longer absorbed into the cloth.
6 If the stain remains, mix one tablespoon of ammonia (caution, see page 33) with two cups of warm water.
7 Sponge the stain with the ammonia solution.
8 Blot until the liquid is absorbed.
9 Sponge with cold water and blot dry.

DEEP-DOWN MILDEW

If moisture and mildew have seeped through to the carpet backing and/or the carpet pad, or you can't thoroughly clean and dry the upholstery, call in the services of a cleaning professional. The presence of mold and mildew in your home can cause serious health problems.

MILDEW & MOLD

FABRIC

1   Take the item outside and brush off as much mildew as possible. This will prevent you from scattering the mold spores in the house.

2   Do one of the following:

    If chlorine bleach is safe for the fabric, launder, using chlorine bleach and the hottest water safe for the fabric.

    If chlorine bleach is not safe for the fabric, soak in oxygen bleach and hot water for at least 30 minutes, and then launder.

3   If possible, take the item outside and let it dry thoroughly in the sunlight.

....

UPHOLSTERY

1   If possible, take the item outdoors and brush off as much mildew as possible. This will prevent you from scattering the mold spores in the house. If this isn't possible, vacuum the surface to draw out more of the mildew. Afterward, replace the vacuum-cleaner bag or remove the canister and clean outside.

2   Mix one cup of ammonia (caution, see page 33) with one cup of cool water.

3   Using a clean white cloth, sponge the stains with the ammonia solution.

4   Blot until the liquid is absorbed.

5   Repeat Steps 3 and 4 until the stain disappears.

6   Sponge with cold water and blot dry to remove the ammonia solution.

7   Dry thoroughly. Use a fan or a hair dryer on the "cool" setting to facilitate drying.

— Your Vacuum & Mold —

When you are changing the vacuum bag after removing mold, do it outdoors so there's no chance of releasing mold spores in your home.

CARPET

If there are mildew stains on the surface of the carpet, you must be careful not to add any more moisture to the area.

1 Vacuum the surface to draw out as much of the mildew as possible. Afterward, replace the vacuum-cleaner bag or remove the canister and clean outside.

2 Vigorously mix one tablespoon liquid laundry detergent and two cups cool water to create a froth of suds.

3 Using a damp cloth, apply the suds to the stained area. Sponge gently. Repeat until the stain disappears.

4 Rinse.

5 Thoroughly dry the area.

MILK

FABRIC

1 Pretreat or soak, using an enzyme laundry product. Soak for at least 30 minutes; soak several hours for older stains.

2 Launder.

UPHOLSTERY

method 1

1 Using a clean white cloth, sponge the stain with a dry-cleaning solvent.

2 Blot until the solvent is absorbed.

3 Repeat Steps 1 and 2 until the stain disappears.

method 2

1 Mix one tablespoon of liquid hand dishwashing detergent with two cups of cool water.

2 Using a clean white cloth, sponge the stain with the detergent solution.

3 Blot until the liquid is absorbed.

4 Repeat Steps 2 and 3 until the stain disappears.

5 Sponge with cold water and blot dry.

CARPET

1 Mix one tablespoon of liquid hand dishwashing detergent with two cups of warm water.

2 Using a clean white cloth, sponge the stain with the detergent solution.

3 Blot until the liquid is absorbed.

4 Repeat Steps 2 and 3 until the stain disappears or is no longer absorbed into the cloth.

5 If the stain remains, mix one tablespoon of ammonia (caution, see page 33) with two cups of warm water.

6 Sponge the stain with the ammonia solution.

7 Blot until the liquid is absorbed.

8 Sponge with cold water and blot dry.

DON'T CRY OVER SPILLED MILK

If you don't clean a milk spill adequately, the telltale smell will soon clue you in that more effort is needed.

MOTOR OIL/GREASE

FABRIC

1 Pretreat with a prewash stain remover.

2 Launder, using the hottest water safe for the fabric.

UPHOLSTERY

1 Scrape off excess oil.

2 Sprinkle baking soda, cornstarch, or other absorbent on the stain. Let stand 10 to 15 minutes, and then vacuum.

3 Using a clean white cloth, sponge the stain with a dry-cleaning solvent.

4 Blot until the solvent is absorbed.

5 Repeat Steps 3 and 4 until the stain disappears.

CARPET

1 Scrape off excess oil.

2 Sprinkle baking soda, cornstarch, or other absorbent on the stain. Let stand 10 to 15 minutes, and then vacuum.

3 Using a clean white cloth, sponge the stain with a dry-cleaning solvent.

4 Blot until the solvent is absorbed.

5 If the stain remains, mix one tablespoon of liquid hand dishwashing detergent and one tablespoon of white vinegar with two cups of warm water. Sponge the stain with this solution. Blot until the liquid is absorbed.

6 Sponge with cold water and blot dry to remove the detergent-vinegar solution.

MUD

FABRIC

1 Let the mud dry, and then brush off as much as possible.
2 Pretreat with a prewash stain remover.
3 Launder.

UPHOLSTERY

1 Let the mud dry, and then vacuum up as much as possible.
2 Mix one tablespoon of liquid hand dishwashing detergent with two cups of cool water.
3 Sponge the stain with a clean white cloth and the detergent solution.
4 Blot until the liquid is absorbed.
5 Repeat Steps 3 and 4 until the stain disappears.
6 Sponge with cold water and blot dry.

CARPET

1 Let the mud dry, and then vacuum up as much as possible.
2 Mix one tablespoon of liquid hand dishwashing detergent with two cups of warm water.
3 Sponge the stain with a clean white cloth and the detergent solution.
4 Blot until the liquid is absorbed.
5 Repeat Steps 3 and 4 until the stain disappears.
6 Sponge with cold water and blot dry.

— Worth a Try —

If the mud stains persist, it's possible that they were caused by an iron-based clay. In that case, treat them as rust stains (see page 210).

MUSTARD

FABRIC

method 1

1 Scrape off excess mustard.
2 Rub glycerin into the stain with your fingertips and let it sit for a few minutes.
3 Rinse with cool water.
4 Launder, using the hottest water and type of bleach (chlorine bleach preferred) safe for the fabric.

method 2

1 Scrape off excess mustard.
2 Flush under cold running water to loosen the stain.
3 Pretreat with a prewash stain remover.
4 Launder, using the hottest water and type of bleach (chlorine bleach preferred) safe for the fabric.

UPHOLSTERY

1 Scrape off excess mustard.
2 Mix one tablespoon of liquid hand dishwashing detergent with two cups of cool water.
3 Using a clean white cloth, sponge the stain with the detergent solution.
4 Blot until the liquid is absorbed.
5 Repeat Steps 3 and 4 until the stain disappears.
6 Sponge with cold water and blot dry to remove the detergent solution.

CARPET

1 Scrape off excess mustard.
2 Mix one tablespoon of liquid hand dishwashing detergent with two cups of warm water.
3 Using a clean white cloth, sponge the stain with the detergent solution.
4 Blot until the liquid is absorbed.
5 Repeat Steps 3 and 4 until the stain disappears.
6 If the stain remains, mix one tablespoon of ammonia (caution, see page 33) with two cups of warm water.
7 Sponge the stain with the ammonia solution.
8 Blot until the liquid is absorbed.
9 Sponge with cold water and blot dry to remove the ammonia solution.

NAIL POLISH

FABRIC

1 Place the fabric facedown on a clean white cloth or paper towels and blot with acetone (caution, see page 32).
2 Rinse with clear water.
3 Repeat Steps 1 and 2 until blotting no longer transfers the stain to the cloth or paper towels.
4 Apply a prewash stain remover.
5 Launder.

UPHOLSTERY

1 Carefully blot up excess polish.

2 Using an eyedropper, apply a small amount of acetone (caution, see page 32) to the stain.

3 Blot immediately.

4 Repeat Steps 2 and 3 until no more stain is removed.

5 Using a clean white cloth, sponge the stain with a dry-cleaning solvent.

6 Blot until the solvent is absorbed.

7 If the stain remains, apply hydrogen peroxide. Use an eyedropper to apply the peroxide directly on the stain.

8 Sponge with cold water and blot dry to remove the hydrogen peroxide.

CARPET

1 Carefully blot up excess polish.

2 Using an eyedropper, apply a small amount of acetone (caution, see page 32) to the stain.

3 Blot immediately.

4 Repeat Steps 2 and 3 until no more stain is removed.

5 Using a clean white cloth, sponge the stain with a dry-cleaning solvent.

6 Blot until the solvent is absorbed.

7 If the stain remains, apply hydrogen peroxide. Use an eyedropper to apply the peroxide directly on the stain.

8 Sponge with cold water and blot dry to remove the hydrogen peroxide.

NAIL-POLISH REMOVER

FABRIC

1 Pretreat with a prewash stain remover.

2 Launder.

UPHOLSTERY

1 Mix one tablespoon of liquid hand dishwashing detergent with two cups of cool water.

2 Using a clean white cloth, sponge the stain with the detergent solution.

3 Blot until the liquid is absorbed.

4 Repeat Steps 2 and 3 until the stain disappears.

5 Sponge with cold water and blot dry.

CARPET

1 Mix one tablespoon of liquid hand dishwashing detergent with two cups of warm water.

2 Using a clean white cloth, sponge the stain with the detergent solution.

3 Blot until the liquid is absorbed.

4 Repeat Steps 2 and 3 until the stain disappears.

5 Sponge with cold water and blot dry.

OIL, COOKING → see COOKING OIL

OIL, MOTOR → see MOTOR OIL/GREASE

OIL, OLIVE → see OLIVE OIL

OIL, VEGETABLE → see VEGETABLE OIL

OINTMENT

FABRIC

1 Scrape off excess ointment.
2 Pretreat with a prewash stain remover.
3 Launder, using the hottest water safe for the fabric.

UPHOLSTERY

1 Scrape off excess ointment.
2 Sprinkle baking soda, cornstarch, or other absorbent on the stain. Let stand for 10 to 15 minutes, and then vacuum.
3 Using a clean white cloth, sponge the stain with a dry-cleaning solvent.
4 Blot until the solvent is absorbed.
5 Repeat Steps 3 and 4 until the stain disappears.

CARPET

1 Scrape off excess ointment.
2 Sprinkle baking soda, cornstarch, or other absorbent on the stain. Let stand for 10 to 15 minutes, and then vacuum.
3 Using a clean white cloth, sponge the stain with a dry-cleaning solvent.
4 Blot until the solvent is absorbed.
5 If the stain remains, mix one tablespoon of liquid hand dishwashing detergent and one tablespoon of white vinegar with two cups of warm water. Sponge the stain with this solution. Blot until the liquid is absorbed.
6 Sponge with cold water and blot dry to remove the detergent-vinegar solution.

OLIVE OIL

FABRIC

1 Pretreat with a prewash stain remover.
2 Launder, using the hottest water safe for the fabric.

UPHOLSTERY

1 Scrape off excess oil.
2 Sprinkle baking soda, cornstarch, or other absorbent on the stain. Let stand 10 to 15 minutes, and then vacuum.
3 Using a clean white cloth, sponge the stain with a dry-cleaning solvent.
4 Blot until the solvent is absorbed.
5 Repeat Steps 3 and 4 until the stain disappears.

CARPET

1 Scrape off excess oil.
2 Sprinkle baking soda, cornstarch, or other absorbent on the stain. Let stand for 10 to 15 minutes, and then vacuum.
3 Using a clean white cloth, sponge the stain with a dry-cleaning solvent.
4 Blot until the solvent is absorbed.
5 If the stain remains, mix one tablespoon of liquid hand dishwashing detergent and one tablespoon of white vinegar with two cups of warm water. Sponge the stain with this solution. Blot until the liquid is absorbed.
6 Sponge with cold water and blot dry to remove the detergent-vinegar solution.

ONION

FABRIC

1 Scrape off excess onion.
2 Flush under cold running water to loosen the stain.
3 Pretreat with a prewash stain remover.
4 Launder, using the hottest water and type of bleach safe for the fabric.

UPHOLSTERY

1 Scrape off excess onion.
2 Mix one tablespoon of liquid hand dishwashing detergent with two cups of cool water.
3 Using a clean white cloth, sponge the stain with the detergent solution.
4 Blot until the liquid is absorbed.
5 Repeat Steps 3 and 4 until the stain disappears.
6 Sponge with cold water and blot dry.

CARPET

1 Scrape off excess onion.
2 Mix one tablespoon of liquid hand dishwashing detergent with two cups of warm water.
3 Using a clean white cloth, sponge the stain with the detergent solution.
4 Blot until the liquid is absorbed.
5 Repeat Steps 3 and 4 until the stain disappears or is no longer absorbed into the cloth.
6 If the stain remains, mix one tablespoon of ammonia (caution, see page 33) with two cups of warm water.
7 Sponge the stain with the ammonia solution.
8 Blot until the liquid is absorbed.
9 Sponge with cold water and blot dry.

ORANGE/JUICE

FABRIC

1 Scrape off excess orange.
2 Flush under cold running water.
3 Launder, using the warmest water and type of bleach safe for the fabric.

UPHOLSTERY

1 Scrape off excess orange.
2 Mix one tablespoon of liquid hand dishwashing detergent with two cups of cool water.
3 Using a clean white cloth, sponge the stain with the detergent solution.
4 Blot until the liquid is absorbed.
5 Repeat Steps 3 and 4 until the stain disappears.
6 Sponge with cold water and blot dry.

....

CARPET

1 Scrape off excess orange.

2 Mix one tablespoon of liquid hand dishwashing detergent with two cups of warm water.

3 Using a clean white cloth, sponge the stain with the detergent solution.

4 Blot until the liquid is absorbed.

5 Repeat Steps 3 and 4 until the stain disappears or is no longer absorbed into the cloth.

6 If the stain remains, mix one table-spoon of ammonia (caution, see page 33) with two cups of warm water.

7 Sponge the stain with the ammonia solution.

8 Blot until the liquid is absorbed.

9 Sponge with cold water and blot dry.

PAINT, LATEX (ACRYLIC/WATER-BASED)

FABRIC

1 Scrape off excess paint.

2 Working from the back of the fabric, vigorously flush the stain under warm running water.

3 Mix a solution of one part liquid hand dishwashing detergent to one part warm water.

4 Sponge the stain with the detergent solution, tamping it vigorously.

5 Rinse.

6 Repeat Steps 4 and 5 until no more paint is removed.

7 If the stain remains, try blotting with acetone (caution, see page 32).

UPHOLSTERY

1 Scrape off excess paint.

2 Mix a solution of one part liquid hand dishwashing detergent to one part cool water.

3 Sponge the stain with the detergent solution, tamping it vigorously.

4 Rinse.

5 Repeat Steps 3 and 4 until no more paint is removed.

6 If the stain remains, try blotting with acetone (caution, see page 32).

CARPET

1 Scrape off excess paint.

2 Starting at the outer edge of the stain, apply acrylic paint and varnish remover (available at hardware and paint stores). Gently scrape away the paint as it softens. Repeat, using the remover sparingly, until you have removed as much paint as possible.

3 If any paint remains, work glycerin into the stain and let it soak for several hours.

4 Sponge the stain with a mild solution of liquid hand dishwashing detergent. Tamp vigorously.

5 Blot until the liquid is absorbed.

6 Sponge with a solution of one part white vinegar to ten parts water.

7 Blot until the liquid is absorbed.

8 Sponge with cold water and blot dry.

CONTAIN THE STAIN

When working on carpet stains, keep the paint and varnish remover from spreading the stain. Otherwise, you may create a new type of stain. To avoid this, work on the individual tufts, carefully applying the remover and working it in so it doesn't spread to the surrounding tufts.

PAINT, OIL-BASED

FABRIC

For fresh stains

1 Scrape off excess paint.

2 Using a clean white cloth, blot up as much paint as possible.

3 Rinse. DO NOT let the fabric dry.

4 Place the stain facedown on a stack of white paper towels or cloths. Blot with turpentine. Tamp the stain to help break up the paint. Repeat, replacing the paper towels or cloth until no more paint can be removed.

5 Treat the remaining stain with liquid hand dishwashing detergent and soak overnight.

6 Rinse well.

7 Launder.

8 If the stain remains, treat with a prewash stain remover and launder again.

For old stains

1 Soften the stain by treating it with the product the paint manufacturer recommends for thinning the paint (check the paint can's label).

2 Once the paint has softened, treat as for fresh stains, Steps 2 through 8 above.

Don't Let the Paint Dry

Treat paint stains as promptly as possible. Once the paint dries, the stain may be impossible to remove.

UPHOLSTERY AND CARPET

For fresh stains

1 Scrape up excess paint.
2 Using a clean white cloth, blot up as much paint as possible.
3 Using a clean white cloth, blot the stain with turpentine. Tamp the stain to help break up the paint.
4 Keep applying turpentine to the stain, tamping and blotting until the paint is removed.
5 Sponge the stain with waterless hand cleaner.
6 Mix one tablespoon of liquid hand dishwashing detergent with two cups of cool water.
7 Using a clean white cloth, sponge the stain with the detergent solution.
8 Blot until the liquid is absorbed.
9 Repeat Steps 7 and 8 until the stain disappears.
10 Sponge with cold water and blot dry to remove the detergent solution.

For old stains

1 Soften the stain by treating it with the product the paint manufacturer recommends for thinning the paint (check the paint can's label).
2 Once the paint has softened, treat as for fresh stains, Steps 2 through 10 above.

THE TOP TEN PICNIC STAINS

Here are the most common picnic stains on fabric and how to treat them.

1 **Barbecue sauce** Working from the back of the stain, flush with cold water. Pretreat with a liquid laundry detergent, tamp the stain, and let stand for several minutes. Rinse well. Sponge the stain with white vinegar, and then rinse well. Pretreat with a prewash stain remover, and then launder. If the stain remains, rub with a liquid laundry detergent, and then soak in warm water for up to 30 minutes. Launder again with fabric-appropriate bleach.

2 **Beer** Sponge the spot with cool water or soak for about 30 minutes in a basin of cool water. Pretreat with a prewash stain remover. Launder. If it's safe for the fabric, add chlorine bleach to the wash.

3 **Blueberries** Flush the stain with cool water. Mix one tablespoon of white vinegar and $1/2$ teaspoon of liquid laundry detergent with one quart of warm water. Soak in this solution for 15 minutes. Rinse with water. If the stain remains, sponge with alcohol and rinse thoroughly. Launder, using chlorine bleach, if it's safe for the fabric.

4 **Catsup** Working from the back of the stain, flush with cold water. Pretreat with a liquid laundry detergent, tamp the stain, and let stand for several minutes. Rinse well. Sponge with white vinegar. Rinse well. Pretreat with a prewash stain remover, and then launder. If the stain remains, rub with a liquid laundry detergent, and then soak in warm water for up to 30 minutes. Launder again with fabric-appropriate bleach.

5 Ice cream Pretreat or soak, using an enzyme laundry product. Soak for at least 30 minutes or several hours for older stains. Launder.

6 Mayonnaise Scrape off the excess mayonnaise. Pretreat with a prewash stain remover. Launder, using the hottest water safe for the fabric.

7 Mustard Scrape off excess. Flush under cold running water to loosen the stain and then pretreat with a prewash stain remover. Alternatively, you can rub glycerin into the stain, let it sit for a few minutes, and then rinse. Launder, using the hottest water and the type of bleach (chlorine bleach preferred) that are safe for the fabric.

8 Soft drinks Sponge the spot with cool water or soak for about 30 minutes in a basin of cool water. Pretreat with a prewash stain remover. Launder. If it's safe for the fabric, add chlorine bleach to the wash.

9 Strawberries Flush the stain with cool water. Mix one tablespoon of white vinegar and $1/2$ teaspoon of liquid laundry detergent with one quart of warm water. Soak in this solution for 15 minutes. Rinse with water. If the stain remains, sponge with alcohol and rinse thoroughly. Launder, using chlorine bleach, if it's safe for the fabric.

10 Suntan lotion Pretreat with a prewash stain remover. Launder, using the hottest water safe for the fabric.

PEANUT BUTTER

FABRIC

1 Scrape off excess peanut butter.
2 Pretreat with a prewash stain remover.
3 Launder, using the hottest water safe for the fabric.

UPHOLSTERY

1 Scrape off excess peanut butter.
2 Using a clean white cloth, sponge the stain with a dry-cleaning solvent.
3 Blot until the solvent is absorbed.
4 Repeat Steps 2 and 3 until the stain disappears.

CARPET

1 Scrape off excess peanut butter.
2 Using an eyedropper, apply a small amount of acetone (caution, see page 32) to the stain.
3 Blot immediately.
4 Using a clean white cloth, sponge the stain with a dry-cleaning solvent.
5 Blot until the solvent is absorbed.
6 If the stain remains, mix one tablespoon of liquid hand dishwashing detergent and one tablespoon of white vinegar with two cups of warm water. Sponge the stain with this solution. Blot until the liquid is absorbed.
7 Sponge with cold water and blot dry to remove the detergent-vinegar solution.

PEAR

FABRIC

1 Scrape off excess pear.
2 Flush under cold running water to loosen the stain.
3 Pretreat with a prewash stain remover.
4 Launder, using the hottest water and the type of bleach that are safe for the fabric.

UPHOLSTERY

1 Scrape off excess pear.
2 Mix one tablespoon of liquid hand dishwashing detergent with two cups of cool water.
3 Using a clean white cloth, sponge the stain with the detergent solution.
4 Blot until the liquid is absorbed.
5 Repeat Steps 3 and 4 until the stain disappears.
6 Sponge with cold water and blot dry.

....

CARPET

1 Scrape off excess pear.

2 Mix one tablespoon of liquid hand dishwashing detergent with two cups of warm water.

3 Using a clean white cloth, sponge the stain with the detergent solution.

4 Blot until the liquid is absorbed.

5 Repeat Steps 3 and 4 until the stain disappears or is no longer absorbed into the cloth.

6 If the stain remains, mix one tablespoon of ammonia (caution, see page 33) with two cups of warm water.

7 Sponge the stain with the ammonia solution.

8 Blot until the liquid is absorbed.

9 Sponge with cold water and blot dry.

PENCIL LEAD

FABRIC

1 Use a soft eraser to remove the excess lead.

2 Pretreat with a prewash stain remover.

3 Launder.

....

UPHOLSTERY

1 Use a soft eraser to remove the excess lead.

2 Mix one tablespoon of liquid hand dishwashing detergent with two cups of cool water.

3 Using a clean white cloth, sponge the stain with the detergent solution.

4 Blot until the liquid is absorbed.

5 Sponge the stain with ammonia (caution, see page 33). Blot until the liquid is absorbed.

6 Repeat Steps 3 through 5 until the stain disappears.
7 Sponge with cold water and blot dry.

CARPET

1 Use a soft eraser to remove the excess lead.
2 Mix one tablespoon of liquid hand dishwashing detergent with two cups of warm water.
3 Using a clean white cloth, sponge the stain with the detergent solution.
4 Blot until the liquid is absorbed.
5 Sponge the stain with ammonia (caution, see page 33). Blot until the liquid is absorbed.
6 Repeat Steps 3 through 5 until the stain disappears.
7 Sponge with cold water and blot dry.

PERFUME

FABRIC

1 Pretreat with a prewash stain remover.
2 Launder.

UPHOLSTERY

1 Blot up excess perfume.
2 Using a clean white cloth, sponge the stain with a dry-cleaning solvent.
3 Blot until the solvent is absorbed.
4 Repeat Steps 2 and 3 until the stain disappears.

....

CARPET

1 Blot up excess perfume.

2 Mix one tablespoon of liquid hand dishwashing detergent and one tablespoon of white vinegar with two cups of warm water.

3 Using a clean white cloth, sponge the stain with the detergent-vinegar solution.

4 Blot until the liquid is absorbed.

5 Sponge with cold water and blot dry.

PERSPIRATION

FABRIC

1 Check to see if the stain has changed the color of the fabric. If so, apply ammonia (caution, see page 33) to fresh stains; white vinegar to old ones. Rinse.

2 Pretreat with a prewash stain remover or rub liquid enzyme detergent into stain.

3 Launder using the hottest water safe for the fabric. Stubborn stains may also respond to chlorine or oxygen bleach in the hottest water safe for the fabric.

....

UPHOLSTERY

1 Mix one teaspoon of liquid hand dishwashing detergent and one tablespoon of ammonia (caution, see page 33) with two cups of cool water.

2 Using a clean white cloth, sponge the stain with the detergent-ammonia solution.

3 Blot until the liquid is absorbed.

4 Mix one tablespoon of liquid hand dishwashing detergent and one tablespoon of white vinegar with two cups of cool water.

5 Sponge the stain with the detergent-vinegar solution.

6   Blot until the liquid is absorbed.

7   Using a clean white cloth, sponge the stain with rubbing alcohol. Blot until the liquid is absorbed.

8   Sponge with cold water and blot dry.

....

CARPET

Although perspiration stains may appear on the back and arms of upholstered furniture, the chances of these stains occurring on your carpet are very slim. In the unlikely event that this happens, use the same method as for upholstery.

PINE RESIN

FABRIC

1   Sponge the stained area with a dry-cleaning solvent; let it air-dry.

2   Soak the stain in a solution of one cup of liquid laundry detergent and a few drops of ammonia (caution, see page 33) for at least 30 minutes.

3   Launder.

....

UPHOLSTERY

1 Using a clean white cloth, sponge the stain with rubbing alcohol.
2 Tamp the stain.
3 Blot until the liquid is absorbed.
4 If the stain remains, sponge with turpentine.
5 Mix one tablespoon of liquid hand dishwashing detergent with two cups of cool water.
6 Sponge the stain with the detergent solution.
7 Blot until the liquid is absorbed.
8 Repeat, with alternating applications of turpentine and detergent solution until the stain disappears.
9 Sponge with cold water and blot dry.

....

CARPET

1 Using a clean white cloth, sponge the stain with rubbing alcohol.
2 Tamp the stain.
3 Blot until the liquid is absorbed.
4 If the stain remains, sponge with turpentine.
5 Mix one tablespoon of liquid hand dishwashing detergent with two cups of warm water.
6 Sponge the stain with the detergent solution.
7 Blot until the liquid is absorbed.
8 Repeat, with alternating applications of turpentine and detergent solution until the stain disappears.
9 Sponge with cold water and blot dry.

POLISH, FURNITURE → see FURNITURE POLISH

POLISH, NAIL → see NAIL POLISH

POLISH, SHOE → see SHOE POLISH

POLLEN

FABRIC

1 Gently shake the garment to remove as much pollen as you can.
2 Use the sticky side of a piece of tape to carefully lift off the remaining particles, or vacuum lightly to pull particles out of the fabric. Avoid rubbing particles in.
3 Pretreat with a prewash stain remover.
4 Launder with added bleach that's safe for the fabric.

UPHOLSTERY

1 Vacuum up the pollen particles.
2 Use the sticky side of a piece of tape to carefully lift off the remaining particles.
3 Using a clean white cloth, sponge the stain with a dry-cleaning solvent.
4 Blot until the solvent is absorbed.
5 Repeat Steps 3 and 4 until the stain disappears.

BRUSHING POLLEN

Don't use your hand to brush off the pollen. You run the risk of rubbing the pollen into the fabric or the carpet fibers rather than brushing it off. In addition, the oils from your skin may set the stain.

Worth a Try

If some pollen still remains, place the item in direct sunlight for a few hours; the stain may disappear.

....

CARPET

1 Vacuum up the pollen particles.

2 Use the sticky side of a piece of tape to carefully lift off the remaining particles.

3 Using a clean white cloth, sponge the stain with a dry-cleaning solvent.

4 Blot until the solvent is absorbed.

5 Repeat Steps 3 and 4 until the stain disappears.

POTATO, MASHED

FABRIC

1 Scrape off excess potato.

2 Flush under cold running water to loosen the stain.

3 Pretreat with a prewash stain remover.

4 Launder, using the hottest water and the type of bleach that are safe for the fabric.

....

UPHOLSTERY

1 Scrape off excess potato.

2 Mix one tablespoon of liquid hand dishwashing detergent with two cups of cool water.

3 Using a clean white cloth, sponge the stain with the detergent solution.

4 Blot until the liquid is absorbed.

5 Repeat Steps 3 and 4 until the stain disappears.

6 Sponge with cold water and blot dry.

CARPET

1 Scrape off excess potato.
2 Mix one tablespoon of liquid hand dishwashing detergent with two cups of warm water.
3 Using a clean white cloth, sponge the stain with the detergent solution.
4 Blot until the liquid is absorbed.
5 Repeat Steps 3 and 4 until the stain disappears.
6 Sponge with cold water and blot dry.

POTATO, SWEET → see SWEET POTATO

PUDDING, CHOCOLATE → see CHOCOLATE

PUDDING, ALL FLAVORS EXCEPT CHOCOLATE

FABRIC

1 Scrape off excess pudding.
2 Pretreat with a prewash stain remover.
3 Launder, using the hottest water safe for the fabric.

UPHOLSTERY

method 1

1 Scrape off excess pudding.
2 Using a clean white cloth, sponge the stain with a dry-cleaning solvent.
3 Blot until the solvent is absorbed.
4 Repeat Steps 2 and 3 until the stain disappears.

method 2

1 Mix one tablespoon of liquid hand dishwashing detergent with two cups of cool water.

2 Using a clean, white cloth, apply the detergent solution to the stained area.

3 Blot until the liquid is absorbed.

4 Repeat, applying and blotting the solution until the stain disappears.

5 Sponge with cold water and blot dry.

....

CARPET

1 Scrape off excess pudding.

2 Mix one tablespoon of liquid hand dishwashing detergent with two cups of warm water.

3 Using a clean cloth, apply the detergent solution to the stained area.

4 Blot until the liquid is absorbed.

5 Repeat Steps 3 and 4 until the stain disappears or is no longer absorbed into the cloth.

6 If the stain remains, mix one teaspoon of ammonia (caution, see page 33) with one cup of warm water.

7 Using a clean white cloth, sponge the stain with the ammonia solution.

8 Blot until the liquid is absorbed.

9 Sponge with cold water and blot dry.

RASPBERRY

FABRIC

1 Flush stain with cool water.

2 Mix one tablespoon of white vinegar and $1/2$ teaspoon of liquid laundry detergent with one quart of cool water. Soak in this solution for 15 minutes.

3 Rinse with water.

4 If the stain remains, sponge with rubbing alcohol and rinse thoroughly.

5 Launder, using chlorine bleach, if safe for the fabric.

UPHOLSTERY

1 Mix one tablespoon of liquid hand dishwashing detergent with two cups of cool water.

2 Using a clean white cloth, sponge the stain with the detergent solution.

3 Blot until the liquid is absorbed.

4 Repeat Steps 2 and 3 until the stain disappears or is no longer absorbed into the cloth.

5 If the stain remains, mix one tablespoon of white vinegar with $2/3$ cup of rubbing alcohol.

6 Using a clean white cloth, sponge the stain with the vinegar-alcohol solution.

7 Blot until the liquid is absorbed.

8 Repeat Steps 6 and 7 until the stain disappears.

9 Sponge with cold water and blot dry.

CARPET

1 Mix one tablespoon of liquid hand dishwashing detergent with two cups of cool water.

2 Using a clean white cloth, sponge the stain with the detergent solution.

3 Blot until the liquid is absorbed.

4 Repeat Steps 2 and 3 until the stain disappears or is no longer absorbed into the cloth.

5 If the stain remains, mix one tablespoon of ammonia (caution, see page 33) with two cups of cold water.

6 Sponge the stain with the ammonia solution.

7 Blot until the liquid is absorbed.

8 Sponge with cold water and blot dry.

RELISH

FABRIC

1 Scrape off excess relish.

2 Flush under cold running water to loosen the stain.

3 Pretreat with a prewash stain remover.

4 Launder, using the hottest water and type of bleach safe for the fabric.

UPHOLSTERY

1 Scrape off excess relish.

2 Mix one tablespoon of liquid hand dishwashing detergent with two cups of cool water.

3 Using a clean white cloth, sponge the stain with the detergent solution.

4 Blot until the liquid is absorbed.

5 Repeat Steps 3 and 4 until the stain disappears.

6 Sponge with cold water and blot dry.

CARPET

1 Scrape off excess relish.

2 Mix one tablespoon of liquid hand dishwashing detergent with two cups of warm water.

3 Using a clean white cloth, sponge the stain with the detergent solution.

4 Blot until the liquid is absorbed.

5 Repeat Steps 3 and 4 until the stain disappears or is no longer absorbed into the cloth.

6 If the stain remains, mix one tablespoon of ammonia (caution, see page 33) with two cups of warm water.

7 Sponge the stain with the ammonia solution.

8 Blot until the liquid is absorbed.

9 Sponge with cold water and blot dry.

RUBBER CEMENT

FABRIC

1 Scrape off excess rubber cement.

2 If some glue residue remains, rub petroleum jelly into the stain and then gently roll off the pieces of rubber cement.

3 Pretreat with a prewash stain remover.

4 Launder.

UPHOLSTERY

1 Scrape off excess rubber cement.
2 Using a clean white cloth, sponge the stain with a dry-cleaning solvent.
3 Blot until the solvent is absorbed.
4 Repeat Steps 2 and 3 until the stain disappears.

CARPET

1 Scrape off excess rubber cement.
2 Using a clean white cloth, sponge the stain with a dry-cleaning solvent.
3 Blot until the solvent is absorbed.
4 Mix one tablespoon of liquid hand dishwashing detergent and one tablespoon of white vinegar with two cups of warm water.
5 Sponge the stain with the detergent-vinegar solution.
6 Blot until the liquid is absorbed.
7 Sponge with cold water and blot dry.

RUST

FABRIC

A commercial rust remover (available in supermarkets and hardware stores) is the best way to remove rust. Because these products contain toxic acids, caution is required. Be sure to read and follow the label directions carefully.

UPHOLSTERY AND CARPET

For small spots, try a commercial rust remover. For large or stubborn spots, call in a professional cleaner.

BLEACH AND RUST ALERT!

NEVER use a product with bleach on a rust stain. It will create a chemical reaction that sets the stain.

SALAD DRESSING, CREAMY OR VINAIGRETTE

FABRIC

1 Pretreat with a prewash stain remover.
2 Launder, using the hottest water safe for the fabric.

UPHOLSTERY

1 Scrape off excess salad dressing.
2 Sprinkle baking soda, cornstarch, or other absorbent on the stain. Let stand 10 to 15 minutes, and then vacuum.
3 Using a clean white cloth, sponge the stain with a dry-cleaning solvent.
4 Blot until the solvent is absorbed.
5 Repeat Steps 3 and 4 until the stain disappears.

CARPET

1 Scrape off excess salad dressing.

2 Sprinkle baking soda, cornstarch, or other absorbent on the stain. Let stand for 10 to 15 minutes, and then vacuum.

3 Using a clean white cloth, sponge the stain with a dry-cleaning solvent.

4 Blot until the solvent is absorbed.

5 If the stain remains, mix one tablespoon of liquid hand dishwashing detergent and one tablespoon of white vinegar with two cups of warm water.

6 Using a white cloth, sponge the stain with the detergent-vinegar solution.

7 Blot until the liquid is absorbed.

8 Sponge with cold water and blot dry.

SALSA

FABRIC

1 Working from the back of the stain, flush with cold water.

2 Pretreat with a liquid laundry detergent; tamp the stain and let stand for several minutes.

3 Rinse well.

4 Sponge with white vinegar.

5 Rinse well.

6 Repeat steps 2 through 5 until you have removed as much stain as possible.

7 Pretreat with a prewash stain remover.

8 Launder.

9 If the stain remains, rub with a liquid laundry detergent, and then soak in warm water for up to 30 minutes. Launder again with fabric-appropriate bleach added, if necessary.

UPHOLSTERY

1 Mix one tablespoon of liquid hand dishwashing detergent with two cups of cool water.
2 Using a clean white cloth, sponge the stain with the detergent solution.
3 Blot until the liquid is absorbed.
4 Repeat Steps 2 and 3 until the stain disappears.
5 Sponge with cold water and blot dry.

CARPET

1 Mix one tablespoon of liquid hand dishwashing detergent with two cups of warm water.
2 Using a clean white cloth, sponge the stain with the detergent solution.
3 Blot until the liquid is absorbed.
4 Repeat Steps 2 and 3 until the stain disappears or no more stain is absorbed into the cloth.
5 If the stain remains, mix one tablespoon of ammonia (caution, see page 33) with $1/2$ cup of warm water.
6 Sponge the stain with the ammonia solution.
7 Blot until the liquid is absorbed.
8 Sponge with cold water and blot dry.

FABRIC

1 Pretreat with a prewash stain remover.

2 Launder, using the warmest water and type of bleach safe for the fabric.

3 If the stain remains, sponge with rubbing alcohol and launder again.

UPHOLSTERY

method 1

1 Using a clean white cloth, sponge the stain with a dry-cleaning solvent.

2 Blot until the solvent is absorbed.

3 Repeat Steps 1 and 2 until the stain disappears.

method 2

1 Mix one tablespoon of liquid hand dishwashing detergent with two cups of cool water.

2 Using a clean white cloth, sponge the stain with the detergent solution.

3 Blot until the liquid is absorbed.

4 Repeat Steps 2 and 3 until the stain disappears.

5 Sponge with cold water and blot dry.

CARPET

1 Using a clean white cloth, sponge the stain with a dry-cleaning solvent.

2 Blot until the solvent is absorbed.

3 Repeat Steps 1 and 2 until the stain disappears.

SCORCH MARKS (LIGHT)

FABRIC

1 Using an eye dropper, apply hydrogen peroxide to the stain. Add a drop or two of ammonia (caution, see page 33).

2 Let it stand from several minutes up to an hour. Don't let the stain dry. Keep it moist with hydrogen peroxide and ammonia.

3 Flush with water.

4 Launder, using oxygen bleach, if safe for the fabric.

QUICK SCORCH TRICKS

If you scorch an item while ironing it, there are two fast and easy ways to repair the damage. The trick is to do one of them immediately.

- If you have time, rub liquid laundry detergent into the scorch mark and launder the item right away, using liquid laundry detergent and oxygen bleach, if safe for the fabric.
- If you need the item immediately and the scorch marks are slight, lightly rub white distilled vinegar on the fabric. Wipe with a clean cloth.

Heavily scorched fabrics where the fibers are burned and damaged can't be returned to their original state; the same is true for melted or shiny areas.

SHAVING CREAM

FABRIC

1 Pretreat with a prewash stain remover.
2 Launder.

UPHOLSTERY

1 Mix one tablespoon of liquid hand dishwashing detergent with two cups of cool water.
2 Using a clean white cloth, sponge the stain with the detergent solution.
3 Blot until the liquid is absorbed.
4 Repeat Steps 2 and 3 until the stain disappears.
5 Sponge with cold water and blot dry.

CARPET

1 Mix one tablespoon of liquid hand dishwashing detergent with two cups of warm water.
2 Using a clean white cloth, sponge the stain with the detergent solution.
3 Blot until the liquid is absorbed.
4 Repeat Steps 2 and 3 until the stain disappears.
5 Sponge with cold water and blot dry.

CREAM OF THE CROP

Shaving cream from a can likely contains more oil than shaving soap, and more care should be applied in removing the strain.

SHOE POLISH

FABRIC

method 1

1 Pretreat with a prewash stain remover.
2 Apply liquid enzyme laundry detergent and tamp the stain.
3 Launder in the hottest water that is safe for the fabric.

method 2

1 Using a clean white cloth, sponge the stain with a dry-cleaning solvent.
2 Blot until the solvent is absorbed.
3 Repeat Steps 1 and 2 until the stain disappears.
4 Launder in the hottest water safe for the fabric.

UPHOLSTERY

1 Scrape off as much polish as possible.
2 Using a clean white cloth, sponge the stain with a dry-cleaning solvent.
3 Blot until the solvent is absorbed.
4 Repeat Steps 2 and 3 until the stain disappears.

CARPET

1 Scrape off as much polish as possible.
2 Sponge the stain with a dry-cleaning solvent.
3 Blot until the liquid is absorbed.
4 Mix one tablespoon of liquid hand dishwashing detergent and one tablespoon of ammonia (caution, see page 33) with two cups of warm water.
5 Using a clean white cloth, sponge the stain with the detergent-ammonia solution.
6 Blot until the liquid is absorbed.
7 Sponge with cold water and blot dry.

SMOKE

FABRIC

1 Pretreat with a prewash stain remover.

2 Launder, using the warmest water and type of bleach safe for the fabric.

3 If the stain remains, sponge with rubbing alcohol and launder again.

UPHOLSTERY

method 1

1 Using a clean white cloth, sponge the stain with a dry-cleaning solvent.

2 Blot until the solvent is absorbed.

3 Repeat Steps 1 and 2 until the stain disappears.

method 2

1 Mix one tablespoon of liquid hand dishwashing detergent with two cups of cool water.

2 Using a clean white cloth, sponge the stain with the detergent solution.

3 Blot until the liquid is absorbed.

4 Repeat Steps 2 and 3 until the stain disappears.

5 Sponge with cold water and blot dry.

CARPET

1 Using a clean white cloth, sponge the stain with a dry-cleaning solvent.

2 Blot until the solvent is absorbed.

3 Repeat Steps 1 and 2 until the stain disappears.

CALL IN THE PROS

Major smoke and soot damage—the kind that occurs in a fire—requires the services of cleaning professionals. Contact your insurance agent immediately for guidance and recommendations. Disaster-restoration companies specialize in this type of cleanup.

SOFT DRINKS

FABRIC

1 Sponge the spot with cool water or soak for about 30 minutes in a basin of cool water.
2 Pretreat with a prewash stain remover.
3 Launder. If it's safe for the fabric, add chlorine bleach to the wash.

....

UPHOLSTERY

method 1

1 Blot up as much of the spilled drink as possible.
2 Mix one tablespoon of liquid hand dishwashing detergent with two cups of cool water.
3 Using a clean white cloth, sponge the stain with the detergent solution.
4 Blot until the liquid is absorbed.
5 Repeat Steps 3 and 4 until the stain disappears.
6 Sponge with cold water and blot dry.

method 2

1 Blot up as much of the spilled drink as possible.
2 Using a clean white cloth, sponge the stain with a dry-cleaning solvent.
3 Blot until the solvent is absorbed.
4 Repeat Steps 2 and 3 until the stain disappears.

CARPET

1 Blot up as much of the spilled drink as possible.
2 Use plain water or mix one tablespoon of liquid hand dishwashing detergent and one tablespoon of white vinegar with two cups of warm water.
3 Using a clean white cloth, sponge the stain with plain water or the detergent-vinegar solution. Apply a little bit at a time, blotting frequently with a dry cloth until the stain disappears.
4 Sponge with cold water and blot dry.

SOOT

FABRIC

1 Pretreat with a prewash stain remover.
2 Launder, using the warmest water and the type of bleach that are safe for the fabric.
3 If the stain remains, sponge with rubbing alcohol and launder again.

UPHOLSTERY

method 1

1 Sprinkle baking soda, cornstarch, or other absorbent on the stain. Let stand at least one hour, and then vacuum.

2 Using a clean white cloth, sponge the stain with a dry-cleaning solvent.

3 Blot until the solvent is absorbed.

4 Repeat Steps 2 and 3 until the stain disappears.

method 2

1 Sprinkle baking soda, cornstarch, or other absorbent on the stain. Let stand at least one hour, and then vacuum.

2 Mix one tablespoon of liquid hand dishwashing detergent with two cups of cool water.

3 Using a clean white cloth, sponge the stain with the detergent solution.

4 Blot until the liquid is absorbed.

5 Repeat Steps 3 and 4 until the stain disappears.

6 Sponge with cold water and blot dry.

CARPET

1 Sprinkle baking soda, cornstarch, or other absorbent on the stain. Let stand at least one hour, and then vacuum.

2 Using a clean white cloth, sponge the stain with a dry-cleaning solvent.

3 Blot until the solvent is absorbed.

4 Repeat Steps 2 and 3 until the stain disappears.

THE TEN STAINS OF CHRISTMAS

Here are the most common Christmas stains on fabric and how to treat them.

1 **Candle wax** If the wax is still soft, freeze to harden, and then scrape off excess. Sponge with a dry-cleaning fluid. Place stain between clean paper towels and press with a warm iron to transfer the wax to the paper towels. Replace the paper towels frequently to absorb more wax and prevent the stain from transferring to other places on the fabric. Pretreat with a prewash stain remover. Launder. If any color remains, rewash using chlorine bleach, if safe for the fabric, or oxygen bleach.

2 **Candy canes** Rinse with warm water. Launder in the warmest water safe for the fabric.

3 **Coffee** Sponge the spot with cool water or soak for about 30 minutes in a basin of cool water. If the stain is old, soak overnight. Pretreat with a prewash stain remover. Launder. If it's safe for the fabric, add chlorine bleach to the wash.

4 **Cranberry sauce** Flush the stain with cool water. Mix one tablespoon of white vinegar and $1/2$ teaspoon of liquid laundry detergent with one quart of warm water. Soak in this solution for 15 minutes; rinse. If the stain remains, sponge with rubbing alcohol and rinse thoroughly. Finally, launder, using chlorine bleach, if safe for the fabric.

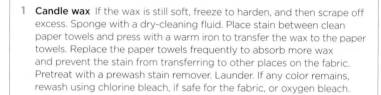

5 **Eggnog** Pretreat or soak for at least 30 minutes, using an enzyme laundry product. If the stain is old, soak for several hours. Launder, using an enzyme laundry detergent.

6 **Gravy** Pretreat with a prewash stain remover. Launder, using the hottest water safe for the fabric.

7 **Pine resin** Sponge with acetone (caution, see page 32) and air-dry. Or sponge with dry-cleaning solvent, air-dry, and then soak for at least 30 minutes in a mixture of one cup of liquid laundry detergent and a few drops of ammonia (caution, see page 33). Launder as usual.

8 **Red food coloring** Use a commercial color remover, following the package directions. Launder. Or, if chlorine bleach is safe for the fabric, mix a solution of $1/4$ cup of chlorine bleach per gallon of cool water and soak for 30 minutes. Rinse, and then launder.

9 **Sweet potatoes** Scrape off excess. Flush under cold running water to loosen the stain. Pretreat with a prewash stain remover. Launder, using the hottest water and type of bleach safe for the fabric.

10 **Wine** Sponge the spot with cool water or soak for about 30 minutes in a basin of cool water. Pretreat with a prewash stain remover. Launder. If it's safe for the fabric, add chlorine bleach to the wash.

SOUR CREAM

FABRIC

1 Pretreat with an enzyme laundry product or soak in a solution of a liquid enzyme laundry detergent and water. Soak for at least 30 minutes or several hours for older stains.

2 Launder.

UPHOLSTERY

method 1

1 Using a clean white cloth, sponge the stain with a dry-cleaning solvent.

2 Blot until the solvent is absorbed.

3 Repeat Steps 1 and 2 until the stain disappears.

method 2

1 Mix one tablespoon of liquid hand dishwashing detergent with two cups of cool water.

2 Using a clean white cloth, sponge the stain with the detergent solution.

3 Blot until the liquid is absorbed.

4 Repeat Steps 2 and 3 until the stain disappears.

5 Sponge with cold water and blot dry.

CARPET

1 Mix one tablespoon of liquid hand dishwashing detergent with two cups of warm water.

2 Using a clean white cloth, sponge the stain with the detergent solution.

3 Blot until the liquid is absorbed.

4 Repeat Steps 2 and 3 until the stain disappears or is no longer absorbed into the cloth.

5 If the stain remains, mix one tablespoon of ammonia (caution, see page 33) with two cups of warm water.

6 Sponge the stain with the ammonia solution.

7 Blot until the liquid is absorbed.

8 Sponge with cold water and blot dry.

SOY SAUCE

FABRIC

1 Flush the stain with cold running water.

2 Sponge with ammonia (caution, see page 33), and rinse until you have removed as much stain as possible.

3 Pretreat with a prewash stain remover.

4 Launder with a fabric-appropriate bleach, if necessary.

UPHOLSTERY

1 Mix one tablespoon of liquid hand dishwashing detergent with two cups of cool water.

2 Sponge the stain with a clean white cloth and the detergent solution.

3 Blot until the liquid is absorbed.

4 Repeat Steps 2 and 3 until the stain disappears.

5 Sponge with cold water and blot dry.

CARPET

1 Mix one tablespoon of liquid hand dishwashing detergent with two cups of warm water.

2 Sponge the stain with a clean white cloth and the detergent solution.

3 Blot until the liquid is absorbed.

4 If the stain remains, mix one tablespoon of ammonia (caution, see page 33) with $1/2$ cup of water.

5 Sponge the stain with the ammonia solution.

6 Blot until the liquid is absorbed.

7 Sponge with cold water and blot dry.

SPAGHETTI SAUCE

FABRIC

1 Working from the back of the stain, flush with cool water.

2 Pretreat with a liquid laundry detergent; tamp the stain and let stand for several minutes.

3 Rinse well.

4 Sponge with white vinegar.

5 Rinse well.

6 Repeat steps 2 through 5 until you have removed as much stain as possible.

7 Pretreat with a prewash stain remover.

8 Launder.

9 If the stain remains, rub with a liquid laundry detergent, and then soak in warm water for up to 30 minutes.

10 Launder again with fabric-appropriate bleach, if necessary.

UPHOLSTERY

1 Using a clean white cloth, apply a dry-cleaning solvent to the stained area.

2 Blot until the liquid is absorbed.

3 Repeat, applying and blotting the solution until the stain disappears or is no longer absorbed onto the cloth.

4 If the stain remains, mix one tablespoon of liquid hand dishwashing detergent with two cups of cool water.

5 Using a clean white cloth, sponge the stain with the detergent solution.

6 Blot until the liquid is absorbed.

7 Repeat Steps 5 and 6 until the stain disappears.

8 Sponge with cold water and blot dry.

CARPET

1 Mix one tablespoon of liquid hand dishwashing detergent with two cups of cool water.

2 Using a clean white cloth, sponge the stain with the detergent solution.

3 Blot until the liquid is absorbed.

4 If the stain remains, mix one tablespoon of ammonia (caution, see page 33) with $1/2$ cup of cool water.

5 Sponge the stain with the ammonia solution.

6 Blot until the liquid is absorbed.

7 Sponge with cold water and blot dry to remove the ammonia solution.

SQUASH

FABRIC

1 Scrape off excess squash.

2 Flush under cold running water to loosen the stain.

3 Pretreat with a prewash stain remover.

4 Launder, using the hottest water and the type of bleach that are safe for the fabric.

UPHOLSTERY

1 Scrape off excess squash.

2 Mix one tablespoon of liquid hand dishwashing detergent with two cups of cool water.

3 Using a clean white cloth, sponge the stain with the detergent solution.

4 Blot until the liquid is absorbed.

5 Repeat Steps 3 and 4 until the stain disappears.

6 Sponge with cold water and blot dry.

....

CARPET

1 Scrape off excess squash.
2 Mix one tablespoon of liquid hand dishwashing detergent with two cups of warm water.
3 Using a clean white cloth, sponge the stain with the detergent solution.
4 Blot until the liquid is absorbed.
5 Repeat Steps 3 and 4 until the stain disappears.
6 Sponge with cold water and blot dry.

STEAK SAUCE

FABRIC

1 Flush the stain with cold running water.
2 Sponge with ammonia (caution, see page 33).
3 Rinse well.
4 Repeat Steps 2 and 3 until you have removed as much stain as possible.
5 Pretreat with a prewash stain remover.
6 Launder with fabric-appropriate bleach, if necessary.

....

UPHOLSTERY

1 Mix one tablespoon of liquid hand dishwashing detergent with two cups of cool water.
2 Using a clean white cloth, sponge the stain with the detergent solution.
3 Blot until the liquid is absorbed.
4 Repeat Steps 2 and 3 until the stain disappears.
5 Sponge with cold water and blot dry.

CARPET

1 Mix one tablespoon of liquid hand dishwashing detergent with two cups of warm water.

2 Using a clean white cloth, sponge the stain with the detergent solution.

3 Blot until the liquid is absorbed.

4 Repeat Steps 2 and 3 until the stain disappears or is no longer absorbed into the cloth.

5 If the stain remains, mix one tablespoon of ammonia (caution, see page 33) with $1/2$ cup of warm water.

6 Sponge the stain with the ammonia solution.

7 Blot until the liquid is absorbed.

8 Sponge with cold water and blot dry.

STRAWBERRY

FABRIC

1 Flush the stain with cool water.

2 Mix one tablespoon of white vinegar and $1/2$ teaspoon of liquid laundry detergent with one quart of cool water. Soak in this solution for 15 minutes.

3 Rinse with water.

4 If the stain remains, sponge with alcohol and rinse thoroughly.

5 Launder, using chlorine bleach, if safe for the fabric.

UPHOLSTERY

1 Mix one tablespoon of white vinegar with $2/3$ cup of rubbing alcohol.
2 Using a clean white cloth, sponge the stain with the vinegar-alcohol solution.
3 Blot until the liquid is absorbed.
4 Repeat Steps 2 and 3 until the stain disappears.
5 Sponge with cold water and blot dry.

CARPET

1 Mix one tablespoon of liquid hand dishwashing detergent with two cups of cool water.
2 Using a clean white cloth, sponge the stain with the detergent solution.
3 Blot until the liquid is absorbed.
4 Repeat Steps 2 and 3 until the stain disappears or is no longer absorbed into the cloth.
5 If the stain remains, mix one tablespoon of ammonia (caution, see page 33) with two cups of cold water.
6 Sponge the stain with the ammonia solution.
7 Blot until the liquid is absorbed.
8 Sponge with cold water and blot dry.

SUNTAN LOTION

FABRIC

1 Scrape off excess lotion.
2 Pretreat with a prewash stain remover.
3 Launder, using the hottest water safe for the fabric.

UPHOLSTERY

1 Scrape off excess lotion.

2 Sprinkle baking soda, cornstarch, or other absorbent on the stain. Let stand 10 to 15 minutes, and then vacuum.

3 Using a clean white cloth, sponge the stain with a dry-cleaning solvent.

4 Blot until the solvent is absorbed.

5 Repeat Steps 3 and 4 until the stain disappears.

CARPET

1 Scrape off excess lotion.

2 Sprinkle baking soda, cornstarch, or other absorbent on the stain. Let stand for 10 to 15 minutes, and then vacuum.

3 Using a clean white cloth, sponge the stain with a dry-cleaning solvent.

4 Blot until the solvent is absorbed.

5 If the stain remains, mix one tablespoon of liquid hand dishwashing detergent and one tablespoon of white vinegar with two cups of warm water.

6 Using a clean white cloth, sponge the stain with the detergent-vinegar solution.

7 Blot until the liquid is absorbed.

8 Sponge with cold water and blot dry.

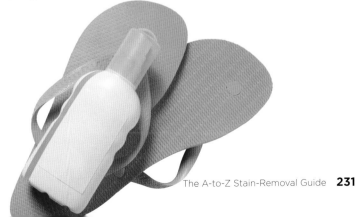

SUPERGLUE

FABRIC

1 If possible, gently scrape off excess superglue.
2 Place fabric face down and sponge with acetone (caution, see page 32).
3 Turn garment faceup and sponge again with acetone.
4 Rinse well.
5 Repeat Steps 2 through 4 until you have removed as much superglue as possible.
6 Pretreat with a prewash stain remover.
7 Launder.

UPHOLSTERY

1 Carefully blot up excess superglue.
2 Using an eye dropper, apply a small amount of acetone (caution, see page 32) to the stain.
3 Blot immediately.
4 Repeat Steps 2 and 3 until no more stain is removed.
5 Using a clean white cloth, sponge the stain with a dry-cleaning solvent.
6 Blot until the solvent is absorbed.
7 If the stain remains, use an eyedropper to apply hydrogen peroxide directly on the stain. Blot dry.

SUPERGLUE SOLUTION

The easiest way to get rid of superglue stains is to purchase commercial superglue remover. If you can't find this type of remover in an office-supply or other store, check the glue manufacturer's website or call for a recommendation.

CARPET

1 Carefully blot up excess superglue.
2 Using an eye dropper, apply a small amount of acetone (caution, see page 32) to the stain.
3 Blot immediately.
4 Repeat Steps 2 and 3 until no more stain is removed.
5 Using a clean white cloth, sponge the stain with a dry-cleaning solvent.
6 Blot until the solvent is absorbed.
7 If the stain remains, use an eyedropper to apply hydrogen peroxide directly on the stain. Blot dry.

SWEAT → see PERSPIRATION

SWEET POTATO

FABRIC

1 Scrape off excess sweet potato.
2 Flush under cold running water to loosen the stain.
3 Pretreat with a prewash stain remover.
4 Launder, using the hottest water and the type of bleach that are safe for the fabric.

UPHOLSTERY

1 Scrape off excess sweet potato.
2 Mix one tablespoon of liquid hand dishwashing detergent with two cups of cool water.
3 Using a clean white cloth, sponge the stain with the detergent solution.
4 Blot until the liquid is absorbed.
5 Repeat Steps 3 and 4 until the stain disappears.
6 Sponge with cold water and blot dry.

CARPET

1 Scrape off excess sweet potato.

2 Mix one tablespoon of liquid hand dishwashing detergent with two cups of warm water.

3 Using a clean white cloth, sponge the stain with the detergent solution.

4 Blot until the liquid is absorbed.

5 Repeat Steps 3 and 4 until the stain disappears or is no longer absorbed into the cloth.

6 If the stain remains, mix one tablespoon of ammonia (caution, see page 33) with two cups of warm water.

7 Sponge the stain with the ammonia solution.

8 Blot until the liquid is absorbed.

9 Sponge with cold water and blot dry.

HOW SWEET IT IS

Sweet potatoes contain more nutrients than their white counterparts, but also a greater potential for causing stains.

TAPE (ADHESIVE RESIDUE)

FABRIC

1 Scrape off excess residue.

2 If some sticky residue remains, rub waterless hand cleaner into the stain and then gently roll off the bits of adhesive.

3 Pretreat with a prewash stain remover.

4 Launder.

UPHOLSTERY

1 Scrape off excess residue.

2 Using a clean white cloth, sponge the stain with a dry-cleaning solvent.

3 Blot until the solvent is absorbed.

4 Repeat Steps 2 and 3 until the stain disappears.

CARPET

1 Scrape off excess residue.

2 Using a clean white cloth, sponge the stain with a dry-cleaning solvent.

3 Blot until the solvent is absorbed.

4 Mix one tablespoon of liquid hand dishwashing detergent and one tablespoon of white vinegar with two cups of warm water.

5 Sponge the stain with the detergent-vinegar solution.

6 Blot until the liquid is absorbed.

7 Sponge with cold water and blot dry.

TAR

FABRIC

1 Scrape off as much tar as possible.
2 Pretreat with a prewash stain remover.
3 Apply liquid enzyme laundry detergent and tamp the stain.
4 Launder in the hottest water that is safe for the fabric.
5 If the stain remains, using a clean white cloth, apply a dry-cleaning solvent to the stained area.
6 Blot until the liquid is absorbed.
7 Repeat, applying and blotting the solution until the stain disappears.
8 Launder again in the hottest water safe for the fabric.

UPHOLSTERY

1 Scrape off as much tar as possible.
2 Using a clean white cloth, sponge the stain with a dry-cleaning solvent.
3 Blot until the solvent is absorbed.
4 Repeat Steps 2 and 3 until the stain disappears.

CARPET

1 Scrape off as much tar as possible.
2 Sponge the stain with a dry-cleaning solvent.
3 Blot until the liquid is absorbed.
4 Mix one tablespoon of liquid hand dishwashing detergent and one tablespoon of white vinegar with two cups of warm water.
5 Sponge the stain with the detergent-vinegar solution.
6 Blot until the liquid is absorbed.
7 Sponge with cold water and blot dry.

TEA

FABRIC

1 Sponge the spot with cool water or soak for about 30 minutes in a basin of cool water.

2 Pretreat with a prewash stain remover.

3 Launder. If it's safe for the fabric, add chlorine bleach to the wash.

UPHOLSTERY

method 1

1 Mix one tablespoon of liquid hand dishwashing detergent with two cups of cool water.

2 Using a clean white cloth, sponge the stain with the detergent solution.

3 Blot until the liquid is absorbed.

4 Repeat Steps 2 and 3 until the stain disappears.

5 Sponge with cold water and blot dry.

method 2

1 Sponge the stain with a clean white cloth and a dry-cleaning solvent.

2 Blot until the solvent is absorbed.

3 Repeat Steps 1 and 2 until the stain disappears.

CARPET

1 Blot up as much of the spilled tea as possible.

2 Use plain water or mix one tablespoon of liquid hand dishwashing detergent and one tablespoon of white vinegar with two cups of warm water.

3 Using a clean white cloth, sponge with plain water or the detergent-vinegar solution. Apply a little bit at a time, blotting frequently with a dry cloth until the stain disappears.

4 If using a detergent-vinegar solution, sponge with cold water and blot dry to remove the solution.

TOBACCO

FABRIC

1 Dampen the stain and rub with a bar of soap. Rinse.
2 Pretreat or soak with an enzyme laundry product for at least 30 minutes.
3 Launder.
4 If the stain remains, launder again using chlorine bleach, if safe for the fabric.

UPHOLSTERY

1 Mix one tablespoon of liquid hand dishwashing detergent with two cups of cool water.
2 Using a clean white cloth, sponge the stain with the detergent solution. Let stand for about 30 minutes.
3 Blot until the liquid is absorbed.
4 Repeat Steps 2 and 3 until the stain disappears.
5 Sponge with cold water and blot dry to remove the detergent solution.
6 For stubborn stains, mix one tablespoon of sodium thiosulfate with one cup of warm water. Apply to the stained area with an eye dropper. Add a few drops of ammonia (caution, see page 33). Blot until the liquid is absorbed.
7 Sponge with cold water and blot dry.

CARPET

1 Using a clean white cloth, sponge the stain with a dry-cleaning solvent.
2 Blot until the solvent is absorbed.
3 If the stain remains, mix one tablespoon of sodium thiosulfate with one cup of warm water. Sponge the stain with this solution. Blot until the liquid is absorbed.
4 Sponge with cold water and blot dry.

TOUGH TOBACCO

For stubborn tobacco stains, let the fabric air-dry, then apply glycerin to the stain and rub lightly. Launder. If the stain remains, mix one tablespoon of sodium thiosulfate with one cup of warm water. Apply to the stained area with an eye dropper. Add a few drops of ammonia (caution, see page 33). Rinse. Launder again.

TOMATO/JUICE/PASTE/SAUCE

FABRIC

1 Working from the back of the stain, flush with cold water.

2 Pretreat with a liquid laundry detergent, tamp the stain, and let stand for several minutes.

3 Rinse well.

4 Sponge with white vinegar.

5 Rinse well.

6 Repeat Steps 2 through 5 until you have removed as much stain as possible.

7 Pretreat with a prewash stain remover.

8 Launder.

9 If the stain remains, rub with a liquid laundry detergent, and then soak in warm water for up to 30 minutes.

10 Launder with fabric-appropriate bleach, if necessary.

UPHOLSTERY

1 Mix one tablespoon of liquid hand dishwashing detergent with two cups of cool water.

2 Using a clean white cloth, sponge the stain with the detergent solution.

3 Blot until the liquid is absorbed.

4 Repeat Steps 2 and 3 until the stain disappears.

5 Sponge with cold water and blot dry.

CARPET

1 Mix one tablespoon of liquid hand dishwashing detergent with two cups of cool water.

2 Using a clean white cloth, sponge the stain with the detergent solution.

3 Blot until the liquid is absorbed.

4 Repeat Steps 2 and 3 until the stain disappears or is no longer absorbed into the cloth.

5 If the stain remains, mix one tablespoon of ammonia (caution, see page 33) with $1/2$ cup of cool water.

6 Sponge the stain with the ammonia solution.

7 Blot until the liquid is absorbed.

8 Sponge with cold water and blot dry.

PROTECT YOUR PLASTIC

The lycopene in tomatoes diffuses into plastic storage containers and leaves a permanent stain. To avoid this, always microwave leftover tomato sauce in a glass dish.

TONER, PRINTER OR COPY MACHINE

FABRIC

1 Vacuum up or shake off any loose toner.
2 Pretreat with or rub in liquid laundry detergent.
3 Tamp the stain.
4 Launder in cold water.

UPHOLSTERY

1 Vacuum up any loose toner.
2 Mix one tablespoon of liquid hand dishwashing detergent with two cups of cold water.
3 Using a clean white cloth, sponge the stain with the detergent solution.
4 Blot until the liquid is absorbed.
5 Repeat Steps 3 and 4 until the stain disappears.
6 Sponge with cold water and blot dry.

CARPET

1 Vacuum up any loose toner.
2 Mix one tablespoon of liquid hand dishwashing detergent with two cups of cold water.
3 Using a clean white cloth, sponge the stain with the detergent solution.
4 Blot until the liquid is absorbed.
5 Repeat Steps 3 and 4 until the stain disappears.
6 Sponge with cold water and blot dry.

TOOLPASTE

FABRIC

1 Pretreat with a prewash stain remover.
2 Launder.

UPHOLSTERY

1 Mix one tablespoon of liquid hand dishwashing detergent with two cups of cool water.
2 Using a clean white cloth, sponge the stain with the detergent solution.
3 Blot until the liquid is absorbed.
4 Repeat Steps 2 and 3 until the stain disappears.
5 Sponge with cold water and blot dry.

CARPET

1 Mix one tablespoon of liquid hand dishwashing detergent with two cups of warm water.
2 Using a clean white cloth, sponge the stain with the detergent solution.
3 Blot until the liquid is absorbed.
4 Sponge with cold water and blot dry.

Recommended by
THE GOOD HOUSEKEEPING RESEARCH INSTITUTE

LIMITED WARRANTY to CONSUMERS · **GOOD · HOUSEKEEPING** Since ★ 1909 REPLACEMENT or REFUND if DEFECTIVE

For pet-urine stains, try Nature's Miracle, a pet–urine–removal product that also has odor removers. You can find it in pet stores and online.

URINE

FABRIC

1 Pretreat or soak in warm water with an enzyme laundry product.
2 Launder, using chlorine bleach if safe for the fabric, or oxygen bleach.

UPHOLSTERY

1 Mix one tablespoon of liquid hand dishwashing detergent with two cups of cool water.
2 Using a clean white cloth, sponge the stain with the detergent solution.
3 Blot until the liquid is absorbed.
4 Repeat Steps 2 and 3 until the stain disappears.
5 If the stain remains, use an eye dropper to apply hydrogen peroxide, and then add a drop or two of ammonia (caution, see page 33).
6 Sponge with cold water and blot dry.

CARPET

1 Mix one tablespoon of liquid hand dishwashing detergent and one tablespoon of white vinegar with two cups of warm water.
2 Using a clean white cloth, sponge the stain with the detergent-vinegar solution.
3 Blot until the liquid is absorbed.
4 If the stain remains, use an eyedropper to apply hydrogen peroxide, and then add a drop or two of ammonia (caution, see page 33).
5 Sponge with cold water and blot dry.

VEGETABLE OIL

FABRIC

1 Pretreat with a prewash stain remover.
2 Launder, using the hottest water safe for the fabric.

UPHOLSTERY

1 Sprinkle baking soda, corn-starch, or other absorbent on the stain. Let stand 10 to 15 minutes, and then vacuum.
2 Using a clean white cloth, sponge the stain with a dry-cleaning solvent.
3 Blot until the solvent is absorbed.
4 Repeat Steps 2 and 3 until the stain disappears.

CARPET

1 If possible, scrape off excess oil.
2 Sprinkle baking soda, cornstarch, or other absorbent on the stain. Let stand 10 to 15 minutes, and then vacuum.
3 Using a clean white cloth, sponge the stain with a dry-cleaning solvent.
4 Blot until the solvent is absorbed.
5 If the stain remains, mix one tablespoon of liquid hand dishwashing detergent and one tablespoon of white vinegar with two cups of warm water.
6 Sponge the stain with detergent-vinegar solution.
7 Blot until the liquid is absorbed.
8 Sponge with cold water and blot dry.

VINEGAR

FABRIC

1 Flush the stain with cold water.
2 Sponge with ammonia (caution, see page 33). Rinse. Repeat until no more stain is removed.
3 Pretreat with a prewash stain remover.
4 Launder.

UPHOLSTERY

1 Mix one tablespoon of white vinegar with $2/3$ cup of rubbing alcohol.
2 Using a clean white cloth, sponge the stained area with the vinegar-alcohol solution.
3 Blot until the liquid is absorbed.
4 Repeat Steps 2 and 3 until the stain disappears.
5 Sponge with cold water and blot dry.

CARPET

1 Blot up as much of the spilled liquid as possible.
2 Mix one tablespoon of liquid hand dishwashing detergent and one tablespoon of white vinegar with two cups of warm water.
3 Using a clean white cloth, sponge the stain with the detergent-vinegar solution. Apply a little bit at a time, blotting frequently with a dry cloth until the stain disappears.
4 Sponge with cold water and blot dry.

THE INSIDE SCOOP ON VINEGAR

White vinegar is on our list of "stain busters," but other vinegars have dyes and additives that can cause stains. Remember, however, that white vinegar is acidic. If you splash it on your clothing, carpet, or upholstery, don't leave it undiluted. Rinse or sponge with cold water, and then blot until the liquid is absorbed.

VOMIT

FABRIC

1 Scrape off excess vomit.
2 Pretreat with a prewash stain remover.
3 Launder, using the hottest water safe for the fabric.

UPHOLSTERY

1 Scrape off excess vomit.
2 Using a clean white cloth, sponge the stain with a dry-cleaning solvent.
3 Blot until the solvent is absorbed.
4 Repeat Steps 2 and 3 until the stain disappears.

CARPET

1 Scrape off excess vomit.
2 Sprinkle baking soda, cornstarch, or other absorbent on the stain. Let stand 10 to 15 minutes, and then vacuum.
3 Using a clean white cloth, sponge the stain with a dry-cleaning solvent.
4 Blot until the solvent is absorbed.
5 If the stain remains, mix one tablespoon of liquid hand dishwashing detergent and one tablespoon of white vinegar with two cups of warm water. Sponge the stain with this solution. Blot until the liquid is absorbed.
6 Sponge with cold water and blot dry to remove the detergent-vinegar solution.

WATER SPOTS

FABRIC

1 Spread out a clean white or light-colored towel on an ironing board.

2 Turn the garment inside out. Place the area with the water spot face down on the towel.

3 Using a wet cloth, moisten the spotted area thoroughly.

4 Set your iron to the appropriate dry setting for the fabric. Iron the dampened area until dry.

5 Shift the stained area to a dry portion of the towel and repeat Steps 3 and 4 until the water spot disappears.

6 If a slight ring remains, turn the garment right side out and rub the affected area with the back of a spoon.

UPHOLSTERY

1 Using a wet cloth, moisten the spotted area.

2 Fold several paper towels until you have a stack about $1/8$ inch thick. Place them on top of the stain and weight them down with a vase or heavy pot.

3 Point a fan or a hairdryer (on the "cool" setting) at the stain so that the force of the air transfers the moisture to the paper towels.

— Steam it Out —

Water spots on fabric, carpet, or upholstery will often disappear when hit with a blast of steam from an iron or garment steamer. Make sure your iron is emitting steam only; if it spurts water, that will only add to the problem.

CARPET

Carpets and rugs generally do not water-spot. This doesn't mean you should ignore water spills, as untreated moisture can be a breeding ground for mildew.

1 Using a clean white cloth, blot up as much of the moisture as possible. If the carpet is very wet, walk on the cloth to hasten the transfer of the liquid.

2 Fold several paper towels until you have a stack about 1/8 inch thick. Cover the damp spot and weight the towels down with a heavy object, such as a vase or pot, and leave it there overnight. As the carpet dries, the moisture will be absorbed into the paper towels.

3 The next day, remove the paper towels and fluff up the carpet with your hands or a soft brush.

WAX → see CANDLE WAX

WINE, RED

FABRIC

1 Sponge the spot with cool water or soak for about 30 minutes in a basin of cool water.

2 Pretreat with a prewash stain remover.

3 Launder. If it's safe for the fabric, add chlorine bleach to the wash.

Wine Away is a commercial stain remover that is effective for red wine, grape juice, pet accidents, coffee, and grease. Treat the stain with Wine Away, following the application instructions on the bottle.

UPHOLSTERY

method 1

1 Blot up as much of the spilled wine as possible.
2 Mix one tablespoon of liquid hand dishwashing detergent with two cups of cool water.
3 Sponge the stain with a clean white cloth and the detergent solution.
4 Blot until the liquid is absorbed.
5 Repeat Steps 3 and 4 until the stain disappears.
6 Sponge with cold water and blot dry.

method 2

1 Using a clean white cloth, sponge the stain with a dry-cleaning solvent.
2 Blot until the solvent is absorbed.
3 Repeat Steps 1 and 2 until the stain disappears.

— Worth a Try —

If all else fails to remove the red wine stain (especially on a white carpet), mix one part hand dishwashing detergent with two parts hydrogen peroxide. Sponge on; blot off. Rinse well. Be sure to test first in an inconspicuous spot to make sure the solution doesn't harm the color of the carpet.

CARPET

1 Blot up as much of the spilled wine as possible.
2 Use plain water or mix one tablespoon of liquid hand dishwashing detergent and one tablespoon of white vinegar with two cups of warm water.
3 Using a clean white cloth, sponge the stain with plain water or the detergent-vinegar solution. Apply a little bit at a time, blotting frequently with a dry cloth until the stain disappears.
4 If using a detergent-vinegar solution, sponge with cold water and blot dry.

WINE, WHITE

FABRIC

1 Sponge the spot with cool water or soak for about 30 minutes in a basin of cool water.
2 Pretreat with a prewash stain remover.
3 Launder. If it's safe for the fabric, add chlorine bleach to the wash.

UPHOLSTERY

method 1

1 Blot up as much of the spilled wine as possible.
2 Mix one tablespoon of liquid hand dishwashing detergent with two cups of cool water.
3 Using a clean white cloth, sponge the stain with the detergent solution.
4 Blot until the liquid is absorbed.
5 Repeat Steps 3 and 4 until the stain disappears.
6 Sponge with cold water and blot dry.

method 2

1 Using a clean white cloth, sponge the stain with a dry-cleaning solvent.

2 Blot until the solvent is absorbed.

3 Repeat Steps 1 and 2 until the stain disappears.

....

CARPET

1 Blot up as much of the spilled wine as possible.

2 Use plain water or mix one tablespoon of liquid hand dishwashing detergent and one tablespoon of white vinegar with two cups of warm water.

3 Using a clean white cloth, sponge the stain with plain water or the detergent-vinegar solution. Apply a little bit at a time, blotting frequently with a dry cloth until the stain disappears.

4 If using a detergent-vinegar solution, sponge with cold water and blot dry.

WORCESTERSHIRE SAUCE

FABRIC

1 Flush the stain with cold running water.
2 Sponge the stain with ammonia (caution, see page 33).
3 Rinse well.
4 Repeat Steps 2 and 3 until you have removed as much stain as possible.
5 Pretreat with a prewash stain remover.
6 Launder.

UPHOLSTERY

1 Mix one tablespoon of liquid hand dishwashing detergent with two cups of cool water.
2 Using a clean white cloth, sponge the stain with the detergent solution.
3 Blot until the liquid is absorbed.
4 Repeat Steps 2 and 3 until the stain disappears.
5 Sponge with cold water and blot dry.

CARPET

1 Mix one tablespoon of liquid hand dishwashing detergent with two cups of warm water.
2 Using a clean white cloth, sponge the stain with the detergent solution.
3 Blot until the liquid is absorbed.
4 Repeat Steps 2 and 3 until the stain disappears or is no longer absorbed into the cloth.
5 If the stain remains, mix one tablespoon of ammonia (caution, see page 33) with $1/2$ cup of warm water.
6 Sponge the stain with the ammonia solution.
7 Blot until the liquid is absorbed.
8 Sponge with cold water and blot dry.

YOGURT

FABRIC

1 Scrape up excess yogurt.
2 Pretreat or soak, using an enzyme laundry product. Soak for at least 30 minutes; soak several hours for older stains.
3 Launder.

UPHOLSTERY

method 1

1 Scrape up excess yogurt.
2 Using a clean white cloth, sponge the stain with a dry-cleaning solvent.
3 Blot until the solvent is absorbed.
4 Repeat Steps 2 and 3 until the stain disappears.

method 2

1 Scrape up excess yogurt.
2 Mix one tablespoon of liquid hand dishwashing detergent with two cups of cool water.
3 Using a clean white cloth, sponge the stain with the detergent solution.
4 Blot until the liquid is absorbed.
5 Repeat Steps 3 and 4 until the stain disappears.
6 Sponge with cold water and blot dry.

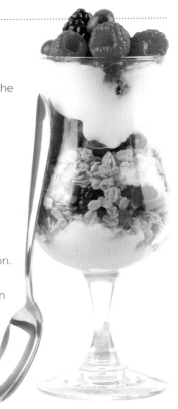

CARPET

1 Scrape up excess yogurt.
2 Mix one tablespoon of liquid hand dishwashing detergent with two cups of warm water.
3 Using a clean white cloth, sponge the stain with the detergent solution.
4 Blot until the liquid is absorbed.
5 Repeat Steps 3 and 4 until the stain disappears.
6 If the stain remains, mix one tablespoon of ammonia (caution, see page 33) with two cups of warm water. Sponge the stain with this solution. Blot until the liquid is absorbed.
7 Sponge with cold water and blot dry.

EXTRAS FOR FRUIT YOGURT

If your yogurt is mixed with fruit, especially berries, take a look at the corresponding instructions before you tackle the stain.

ZUCCHINI

FABRIC

1 Scrape off excess zucchini.
2 Flush under cold running water to loosen the stain.
3 Pretreat with a prewash stain remover.
4 Launder, using the hottest water and the type of bleach that are safe for the fabric.

UPHOLSTERY

1 Scrape off excess zucchini.
2 Mix one tablespoon of liquid hand dishwashing detergent with two cups of cool water.
3 Using a clean white cloth, sponge the stain with the detergent solution.
4 Blot until the liquid is absorbed.
5 Repeat Steps 3 and 4 until the stain disappears.
6 Sponge with cold water and blot dry.

CARPET

1 Scrape off excess zucchini.
2 Mix one tablespoon of liquid hand dishwashing detergent with two cups of warm water.
3 Using a clean white cloth, sponge the stain with the detergent solution.
4 Blot until the liquid is absorbed.
5 Repeat Steps 3 and 4 until the stain disappears.
6 If the stain remains, mix one tablespoon of ammonia (caution, see page 33) with two cups of warm water.
7 Sponge the stain with the ammonia solution.
8 Blot until the liquid is absorbed.
9 Sponge with cold water and blot dry.

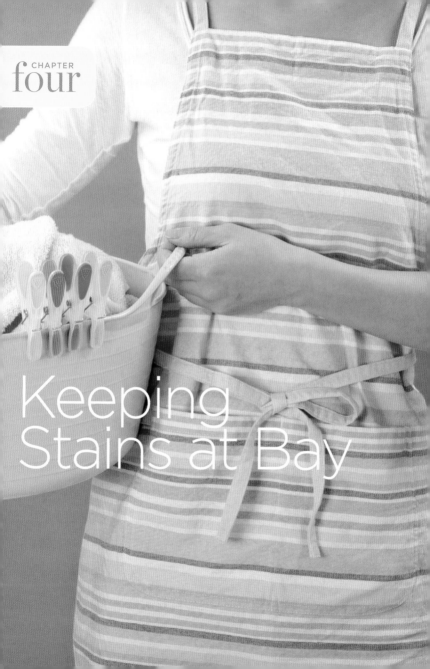

Keeping
Stains at Bay

When it comes to stains, "The best offense is a good defense" is not a cliché. If you can keep a stain from taking hold, you won't have to worry about how to get rid of it. Some stain-prevention measures are simply common sense, while others require a little bit of effort. This isn't a bad tradeoff. Just think about how much time and money you could save by preventing stains! This chapter contains a laundry basket of ideas for keeping stains at bay.

Take-along Treatments

Thanks to new product innovations, stain treatment doesn't have to wait until you get to the laundry room. Products that can travel with you—in the glove compartment, diaper bag, suitcase, backpack, picnic basket, and beach tote—make stain removal easier.

Some of these products function as a prewash. This means they hold the stain in laundry limbo until you can wash the item properly.

STAIN STICKS Stains can be treated and then laundered any time within a week.

WATERLESS HAND CLEANERS Available as gel or foam, these alcohol-based products can work as a prewash for oil and grease stains. Work the gel or foam into the fabric and then remove it with warm water.

Other products are designed to remove most stains completely; they are not just pretreatment products. If the stain remains, you'll need to pretreat the stain as usual before washing the garment at home.

STAIN-REMOVAL WIPES These disposable wipes are designed to treat stains on contact. They can be applied to a garment while you are still wearing it and are safe for most dry-cleanable fabrics.

STAIN-REMOVER PENS These products, which resemble felt-tip pens, come in a variety of formulas. Some may work on greasy stains; others do not. Some need a bit of water to activate the cleaner. If the treated area will be exposed to sunlight, you may want to wipe the stained area with a damp cloth or napkin to get rid of excess solution.

Daily Prevention

Stains are inevitable. But there are all sorts of ways to make sure stains and soils fall on items that are better suited to easy cleaning and easy disposal.

APRONS Thanks to celebrity chefs and cable TV stations devoted exclusively to the culinary arts, Grandma's aprons have come out of the cupboard to become a chic accessory. But let's not overlook the reason she wore them in the first place: to keep spills and stains from invading her clothes.

BIBS So obvious, they almost don't bear mentioning. Moms know how important bibs are, but if a small child is only occasionally in your care, you just might forget. If you don't regret the lapse, the person who does the laundry certainly will! If small children are visitors to your household, keep a few bibs on hand.

DIRT BARRIERS AT THE DOOR

Put an all-weather, hose-down-to-clean doormat outside every entrance to your home. Then put a (preferably washable) rug just inside each door. These easy-to-clean mats and rugs will catch the dirt and keep it from being tracked onto the more expensive and difficult-to-clean carpets in your home. Paired with regular and thorough vacuuming, these dirt barriers are the most important things you can do to prolong the good looks and life of your carpet.

HEADREST AND ARMREST COVERS

When you purchase an upholstered chair or sofa, it usually comes with a set of headrest and armrest covers in matching fabric. These are designed to protect the backs and arms of the furniture from stains caused by body oil, perspiration, and hair products. They are removable, so the covers are easier to clean than the upholstered item itself. However, because the covers absorb a great deal of stain and wear, they tend to look shoddy long before the rest of the upholstery wears out.

There's a simple solution. When you are buying the chair or sofa, ask if you can order a second set of headrest and armrest covers. Rather than using one set until it is worn and then replacing it with the other, switch them. When one set goes off to be cleaned, put the other set on. Continue rotating them so that both sets of covers wear out at approximately the same rate. This way, you won't end up putting bright new covers on upholstery that has begun to fade.

NAPKINS

If paper is your preference, buy the big dinner size—the ones that will completely cover a diner's lap. The money you spend on better, thicker napkins is money you will save on dry-cleaning solvents and prewash stain removers.

SCARVES Wearing a neck scarf inside your coat will protect the collar area of the coat from perspiration, body oils, and hair products.

THROWS Throws are a fashionable room accessory. Just toss one over the dog's favorite chair. Or cover the chair that your kids like to sprawl on. When company comes, fold it neatly and drape it over the chair or, better yet, just whisk it out of sight.

But beware! Many throws are dry-clean only. Washable ones are easier and less expensive to care for.

Small-fry Stains

Kids and stains go hand in hand. Bibs are one way to keep the stains in check, but kids quickly graduate from the bib-and-high-chair stage, and other measures are needed.

Choosing Juice

If you pay attention to the color of the juice you serve your kids, stain removal will be easier. Any juice that has an intense color—such as purple grape juice, cranberry juice, orange juice, tomato juice, and some blended juices—is especially hard to remove because of the dye. When it's laundry time, these stains will require some type of pretreatment and maybe even bleach.

On the other hand, if you encourage your kids to develop a taste for juices that are less intense in color—such as white grape juice, grapefruit juice, and apple juice—stain removal is automatically easier. All that's generally required to remove these stains is to launder the items, using the warmest water safe for the fabric and the type of bleach that's recommended on the care label.

Of course, since these "light" stains are harder to see, they are also easier to overlook. If left untreated for too long, they may start to oxidize and turn brown. If you know juice has spilled on an item, treat it promptly so you won't forget about it.

— Worth a Try —

What works with kids can work with grown-ups, too. White wine stains are much easier to remove than red wine stains. Keep this in mind when planning the menu for your next adult gathering.

Craft Crimes

Crayons, marking pens, finger paints, acrylic paints, colored clay: The craft supplies that spur kids' creativity can be a huge source of stains. But there's an easy way out. Most of these craft supplies come in water-soluble versions. If the color comes off little hands and onto the clothes, it will all come out in the wash!

The ink from permanent marking pens is almost—in some cases, absolutely—impossible to remove. Store these stain culprits far away from your budding Picassos.

Stain Barriers

Whether you call them soil retardants or fabric protectors, the goal is the same: to create an invisible barrier between the fabric and the stains that are trying to attack it. Fabric protectors won't entirely prevent stains, but they will help repel them. They're especially useful for things like the cushions on your kitchen chairs, the necktie that's a magnet for food stains, and the sofa the dog likes to curl up on.

Do-it-yourself Protection

Do-it-yourself fabric protectors come in aerosol and spray pump versions and are available in supermarkets, pharmacies, and hardware stores. Read the label before using any of these products to make sure it is recommended for your specific fabric. Generally they are safe to use on cotton, wool, synthetic fabrics such as polyester and nylon, and delicate fabrics like silk. These products are not usually recommended for rugs, carpets, suede, plastics, or vinyl. For upholstery, compare the upholstery cleaning code with the information on the fabric protector's label. Generally, it is safe to use a fabric protector if the upholstery cleaning code is W, S, or WS. No matter what the various care and content labels say, it is a good idea to test the product in an inconspicuous spot for color bleeding or spotting.

Economically, it makes sense to use these products for small areas, such as chair cushions, garments, seat covers, table runners, and small area rugs. For larger expanses of carpet and fully upholstered pieces, a professional service is the better way to go.

Since men's ties seem to have a special affinity for foods like tomato sauce, soup, and gravy, some fabric protectors are merchandised as tie sprays. These are packaged in convenient carry-along containers. Check the label: It should say the product is safe for silk and that it will not cause colors to bleed. One canister will coat about eight ties. Eventually the protection will wear off. Once the ties are dry-cleaned, they will need to be recoated with protector.

Manufacturer Protection

Fabric protectors can be applied to carpeting and upholstery fabrics at the mill as part of the manufacturing process. How long this built-in soil and stain protection lasts depends on the amount of wear and tear the item receives and how often it is cleaned. At some point, you may have to consider having protection applied to the item by an upholstery and carpet-care professional.

Even apparel fabrics are getting in on the act. Work wear and outdoor wear were the first clothing categories to offer soil and stain protection. Several manufacturers now offer men's casual trousers that are stain repellent. And children's clothing manufacturers are joining in. Can Little League uniforms be far behind?

Professional Protection

Ground-in dirt can wear out carpet and upholstery fabrics long before their time. It's a good idea to treat these items to a deep professional cleaning every 12 to 24 months.

When you are researching a professional to deep-clean your carpets and upholstery, ask about soil and stain protectors that can be applied as part of the cleaning process. If you've purchased carpeting or upholstered furniture that is not treated to resist soils and stains, this is the time to do something about it, though these after-market treatments generally don't last as long as those applied at the factory.

FINDING A PROFESSIONAL

When you hire someone to clean and protect your carpets and upholstery, be sure you get a qualified professional.

- The easiest way to start your search is to ask friends for recommendations. Another way is to contact The Institute of Inspection, Cleaning, and Restoration Certification (800-835-4624). Or go to www.iicrc.com, where you'll find a list of 4,000 members, searchable by zip code.

- Get references—and check them out. Comments from previous customers are the best way to learn about the quality of a company's service.

- Contact your local Better Business Bureau to make sure no one has filed complaints against the company.

- Get a written estimate. This should include an itemized list of the services that will be provided. Spot cleaning and detergent should be included in the basic price. If these are listed as separate charges, keep looking for another cleaner! Legitimate additional charges would be for repairs, deodorization, and fabric or carpet protection.

- Ask for a copy of the cleaner's certificate of insurance. If the cleaner breaks your prized vase, bangs up your walls, or does any other damage, you want to be sure you will be reimbursed. The company should be insured for liability and carry workers' compensation insurance on its employees.

Custom Lamination

There are companies that can apply a soft vinyl protective shield to by-the-yard fabric. The laminate contains a mildew inhibitor to discourage mold and mildew, and a UV inhibitor for protection from sun damage. The laminated, wipe-clean fabric can be used for items such as upholstery, tablecloths, outdoor cushions and furniture, shower curtains, and window shades. Once the fabric is laminated, you have two choices: sew the item yourself or find a professional to sew it for you.

The lamination process works best on bright screen-printed fabrics like cotton chintz; textured fabrics are generally not good candidates. Although the companies that offer this service often require a substantial order, some will process a one-yard test piece at minimal or no cost.

To find a resource, check your local Yellow Pages or do an Internet search for "fabric laminating services."

Stain-free Storage

All textile items, including clothing and linens, should be laundered or dry-cleaned before you store them. Otherwise, food stains can attract bugs that harm the fabric. In fact, small holes are signs that moths, beetles, and other insects may have been enjoying a snack at your not-so-clean wardrobe's expense.

Even items that look spotless should be cleaned. "Invisible" stains, if left untreated, can oxidize during storage and show up as brown or yellow spots that may be impossible to remove.

Clothes should be stored clean but not starched or ironed. Starch and spray fabric finishes will provide insects with the ingredients for a nice meal!

Don't store items in plastic dry-cleaning bags. The bags often break down and damage garments. High-quality plastic garment storage bags are fine. Regular cardboard boxes are not recommended. Instead, store garments in acid-free cardboard boxes in a dark place that has a consistent temperature. Under the bed is a perfect location; the attic, garage, and basement are not good choices. The attic gets too hot. Emissions from a garage or furnace may produce fume damage, which shows up as discoloration on the fabric. Basements are often damp, which may cause mildew damage and a musty smell that's very difficult to remove.

Preventing Mold and Mildew

Towels and bath mats can be mold magnets. Don't let family members get in the habit of leaving damp towels in a heap on the floor. Loosely hang towels and bath mats to air-dry after each use and launder them at least once a week. The same goes for gym clothes and other items that are damp with perspiration. They should go into the laundry immediately or hung to air-dry before being tossed in the hamper.

Mold and mildew are more than just cosmetic issues. If allowed to take hold in your home, they can cause serious health problems.

Keeping things clean—which is what this book is all about—is an important step in preventing the growth of mold and mildew. When moisture and temperature conditions are right, soil on articles can supply the nutrients for mildew to begin to grow. Closets, dresser drawers, basements, and so on should be kept as clean as possible.

Properly installed air-conditioning systems, dehumidifiers in damp areas (especially basements), and exhaust fans in the kitchen and bathrooms will help pull moisture out of the room. Because warm air holds more moisture than cool air (think how much heavier the air feels when it rains on a warm summer day as opposed to a cool winter day), another trick is to turn on the heat in the house for a short period of time to get rid of dampness and then open the doors and windows so the warm, moisture-laden air can escape.

During prolonged periods of wet weather, poorly ventilated closets can be a breeding ground for mold and mildew. To help remove the moisture, get the air moving inside the closet. Open the closet door. Install a small electric fan. Hang clothes loosely so the air can circulate around them.

If the problem persists, you may want to use chemical means, such as moisture-absorbing silica gel, activated alumina, or anhydrous calcium sulfate to remove the dampness from your closet. These chemicals can hold half their weight in water while still feeling dry to the touch. They are also not harmful to fabrics. To use them, hang a cloth bag containing the chemical inside the closet. Or place the chemical in an open container and store it on a shelf (high enough to be well out of the reach of children and pets). The closet door should be well sealed and kept tightly closed so moisture doesn't creep in. Moisture-absorbing chemicals and products are available at home centers and storage retailers.

If the mold and mildew persist, engage the services of a professional. Serious mold and mildew problems require more than a do-it-yourself effort. The source of the moisture must be located and repaired.

TLC for
Heirloom
Textiles

W hether your heirloom textiles are satisfying flea-market finds or treasured family pieces, they need special care. Of course, if you bought a dozen old linen napkins at a garage sale and you plan to use them for holiday occasions, your care routine will be different from that for a precious christening dress you want to bequeath to subsequent generations.

Evaluating Your Textile

The information in this chapter applies to washable heirlooms, specifically linens and cottons. It's up to you to determine the sentimental and monetary value of each piece and plan your care routine accordingly. But you may want to call on some experts for guidance. If your local museum has a textile curator, you may want to solicit his or her advice on the age, fiber content, and care of your piece.

Laundry Products

Keeping these items clean is key to preserving them for a long time. Most of the products discussed in Chapter 2, "First Aid for Stains," can be used on antique cottons and linens. However, there are cautions.

Use a detergent that is free of additives.

This means no bleach, no brighteners, no softeners, and no fragrances, all of which contain chemicals that may damage the fibers. They are also difficult to rinse out completely, which is a special consideration if you plan to store your heirloom textiles for any length of time.

If you are laundering old lace (or taking a chance on washing an old piece of silk or wool), use baby shampoo or a commercial product specially formulated for antique textiles.

Use chlorine bleach as a last resort.

Chlorine bleach is hard on old fibers—it can weaken them, which will hasten decline. So although chlorine bleach may take stains out, it can leave holes in their place. In addition, if a stain is rust, chlorine bleach will set it and make it impossible to remove.

Laundering Techniques

Choose the technique that works best for the age and condition of your fabric.

Somewhat Safe: Machine Wash on the Delicate Cycle

If the item is neither very old nor very fragile, you can wash it on the delicate cycle of your washing machine. For anything more fragile than a linen napkin, consider using a mesh laundry bag (the type that is sold for laundering lingerie). The bag should be large enough to allow the item to move around freely.

Safer: By Hand

Wash by hand in a basin of cool water. Gently move the item around. Rinse by letting the cold water run over it. Do not squeeze, twist, or wring. When the item is thoroughly rinsed, support it carefully as you remove it from the water bath. Place it on a terry-cloth towel and blot gently. Then gently roll it in another towel to remove more of the moisture. Let the item air-dry.

Safest: Soak

Fill a basin, a sink, a bucket, or a laundry tub with warm water. Add baby shampoo or a laundry detergent specially formulated for antique textiles—one to two tablespoons per gallon of water. Agitate the water to disperse the detergent. Gently lower the textile item into the water until it is submerged. Do not move the item around. Just let it soak for hours. Every so often—and ever so gently—move the item around in the water. If the water gets dirty, remove the item. Replace the water and cleaning product and submerge again.

To rinse the item, fill the basin with cold water, submerge the item, and move it gently around in the water. Remove the item, discard the water, and repeat as many times as necessary until you are sure all traces of the detergent have been removed.

Warning: Fabric gets heavier when it is wet. If your heirloom item is particularly fragile, some extra support may be required as you place it into and lift it out of its water bath. An old sheet or a large piece of netting works well as a sling.

SURFACE-DIRT SECRET

Old linens often have a layer of surface dirt that needs to be removed before you can really assess the condition of the fabric or the amount of staining. Soaking is the best way to get rid of this surface dirt.

Bleaching Techniques

If laundering doesn't remove the stains, you may have to resort to a bleaching technique.

Somewhat Safe: Chlorine Bleach

If you know for certain that the stains in question are not rust, and if removing the stain takes priority over preserving the item, soak the item in a solution of ten parts water to one part chlorine bleach. Check it regularly. Remove it from the solution as soon as the stain disappears. Rinse with a white-vinegar-and-water solution. Rinse again with plain water. If an overnight soak doesn't remove the stain, stop trying.

Safer: Oxygen Bleach

Soak the item in a solution of one gallon of cool water with $1/4$ cup of liquid dishwashing detergent and $1/4$ cup of oxygen bleach. Soak overnight to several days. Rinse several times with plain water.

Safest: Grassing or Sun Bleaching

One of the safest techniques for bleaching precious textiles is a very old one called "grassing." But it requires an expanse of grass that is exposed to the sunlight and safe from pets, wildlife, and human traffic. If you have that, the technique is easy.

- Wash the item in a detergent with no additives.

- Roll it in a towel to remove excess moisture.

- While still damp, spread it out on the grass in the direct sunlight. The sun and grass form nitrogen, which bleaches and whitens the fabric.

- For stubborn stains, regularly moisten the fabric by lightly misting it with water from a spray bottle so that it will continue to dry over several days.

Note: If the piece is very old and valuable, too much sun can damage it. Lay it out in filtered sunlight for no more than 10 to 15 minutes. If that doesn't do the trick, either consult a textile specialist or just accept the stains as part of the item's heritage.

Drying

Before choosing your drying method, if you have hand washed the item, roll it up in a towel and press gently to remove the excess moisture.

Then dry it one of the following two ways. (If the item is very fragile or you won't be around to remove it from the dryer while it is still damp, choose the dry-flat method.)

- In the dryer, on a low setting, until it is just slightly damp. Take it out and give it a good shake to remove the wrinkles. Iron it while it is still damp or let it air-dry.

- Dry it flat on an absorbent surface, such as a towel, or on a flat-mesh sweater drying rack. Use your hands to gently smooth out the fabric, removing as many wrinkles as possible. If desired, iron the item before it dries completely.

Never hang heirloom textiles to dry. This means no clotheslines, clothespins, drying racks, or hangers. All of these cause stress on the fabric.

THE SCOOP ON STARCH

You may want to delay ironing until just before you use the item. This way you won't be tempted to use starch, which can attract fiber-eating insects and hasten the breakdown of aged fibers.

Ironing

Heirloom textiles by definition are 100 percent natural fibers—most often linen, cotton, or silk—all of which tend to wrinkle. So fans of heirloom textiles have to love—or at least tolerate—ironing.

The key to successful ironing is to start with an item that is uniformly damp. If you've let the item dry completely—or if you've taken the unironed item out of storage—here's how to dampen it:

1 Mist it with water.

2 Roll it up.

3 Put it in a terry-cloth towel, roll up the towel, and store it in the refrigerator for a few hours.

4 When you're ready to iron, take the towel-wrapped item out of the refrigerator and unroll it. Let it air out for about five minutes before ironing.

Iron with care. Be particularly cautious when ironing over areas with antique lace. Hold the iron over the lace and gently steam it. Placing the iron flat on the lace can cause it to loose some of its "loft"; moving the iron back and forth over the lace can distort its shape. Lace should be ironed over a towel, for cushioning.

Storage

All textiles, regardless of age, should be stored clean and unironed even if the item was used or worn for only a short time. Otherwise, stains from body oils may appear during storage.

When it comes to long-term storing of textiles, all the experts agree on one thing: NO PLASTIC BAGS. They can trap damp air, creating a breeding ground for mold and mildew. They can emit harmful vapors that will break down the fibers.

Special Supplies

Containers and wrappings for heirloom textiles should be acid-free. Here's why: Over time, the natural acids found in most wood and wood products (which includes cardboard, wrapping paper, and tissue paper) will leach out of the wood or wood product and onto the fabric, causing yellowing and staining.

ACID-FREE TISSUE PAPER comes in two versions:

Unbuffered—safe for all natural fibers: cotton, linen, silk, and wool

Buffered—safe for cotton and linen but too alkaline for silk and wool

Resist the temptation to store your precious textiles in lovely colored tissue paper. Besides not being acid-free, colored tissue paper contains dye that can migrate onto your fabric.

ACID-FREE BOXES For long-term storage of precious textiles, acid-free boxes are a good way to go. They come in a variety of sizes so you can store items individually or in small quantities. This keeps layers of fabric from pressing down on each other—another potential source of harm.

Sources for acid-free products include art-supply stores and dry-cleaners, as well as companies that specialize in archival supplies and textile conservation. Storage-supply stores and museum shops also sometimes carry these products. If you can't locate a source near you, an Internet search should turn up sources.

PH PEN If you are in doubt about the acid-free quality of your boxes or tissue paper, a pH pen is the helper you need. When first applied to a paper product, a small dot of the ink from this pen is blue. If the paper is acid-free, the color stays blue. If there is any acid, the color will change to green. If there is a lot of acid, the color will change to yellow.

Over time, even acid-free tissue paper and boxes may absorb acids from the atmosphere. If you've stored something in the same box or with the same tissue paper for at least ten years, use a pH pen to check the tissue and the box. If any acid is indicated, replace them with new tissue and containers. It's a good idea to periodically check on stored items.

Companies that carry archival supplies usually carry pH pens.

Containers

Suitcases, regular cardboard boxes, and plastic bins are no-nos. Here's what's on the "yes" list.

ACID-FREE BOXES As noted earlier, this is the preferred way to store heirloom textiles. The downside of these boxes is that they can be expensive.

CLEAN WHITE COTTON OR LINEN PILLOWCASES Before using pillowcases for storage, wash them in an additive-free detergent and then run them through the rinse cycle twice. During storage, check pillowcases regularly for signs of yellowing or browning. At the first hint of this type of discoloration, rewash and rinse the pillowcase. (When you remove the contents, check them, too, for signs of discoloration. Rewash, if necessary.) Move the rewashed pillowcase with its contents to a different piece of furniture or acid-free box.

MUSLIN YARDAGE OR WHITE SHEETS These can be used instead of acid-free tissue paper to wrap items for storage. Launder as for pillowcases and check regularly for signs of yellowing or browning.

WOOD DRAWERS LINED WITH ACID-FREE TISSUE PAPER The tissue paper is essential. Without it, the acid in the wood will turn your clean textiles yellow or brown—at a rate you may find alarming.

Warning: Cedar chests pose problems for linen and cotton. The oil in the cedar can cause brown spots on these fabrics. For extra protection, line the chest with buffered acid-free tissue paper or muslin. Then wrap the items in muslin or put them in a pillowcase before storing them in the chest.

Location

Since heirloom textiles are more fragile than your general wardrobe, the requirements for storing them are stricter than those for seasonal storage. Here are the optimal conditions.

NO LIGHT Sunlight and artificial light cause deterioration in natural fibers and can also cause dyes to fade.

CONSTANT TEMPERATURE Places that have fluctuating temperature, such as attics and basements, are not good choices. The optimum temperature range is 68º–70ºF (20º–21ºC).

MODERATE HUMIDITY High humidity fosters mold and mildew. Low humidity can dry out fibers, making them brittle. The best storage environment has 50 to 55 percent relative humidity.

Special Considerations

No matter where you store your items or what you store them in, here are some TLC tips.

- If it's necessary to stack the items, place the heavier things on the bottom, lighter ones on top.

- When folding and putting away clean items, be sure your hands are clean and and free of lotions and oils.

- Store items as flat as possible.

- If you don't use your linens regularly, schedule a once-a-year checkup for spots and stains.

- If you store things folded, take them out and refold them occasionally so the creases are in different spots. This takes the stress off the folds and keeps the fibers from splitting along the creases.

- To avoid crease marks altogether, stuff the folds with acid-free tissue paper.

- If the item is a garment that will be worn with some regularity, hang it on a padded hanger and cover with a clean sheet or clean muslin. Never hang knits, heavy beaded garments, or garments cut on the bias, as they can stretch. Instead, store them folded.

Index

Photography Credits

Alamy
Stephen Barnes/Lifestyle, 10 (bottom)

Mediablitzimages, 134

Presselect, 185

Corbis images
JGI/Jamie Grill/Blend Images, 51

Vstock LLC/Tetra Images, 47

Getty images
Amana Productions, 237

Armstrong Studios, 84

Arthur S. Aubry, 177

Brand X Pictures, 223

Rosemary Calvert, 221

Jeffrey Coolidge, 172

Lilli Day, 116

Nick M Do, 208

Dreamlight, 119

Harrison Eastwood, 227

Don Farrall, 203

Marc O. Finley, 154

Foodcollection, 99, 187, 205

Jules Frazier, 110

Fuse, 18, 168

Joop Greypink, 245

Brian Hagiwara, 11 (bottom)

Nicole Hill, 16

Imagesource, 58, 195

Peter LaMastro, 259

Dorling Kindersley , 222 (bottom), 224

Steve Korn, 53

Ryan McVay, 46

MIXA, 48

Photonica, 11 (top), Tim Ridley, 181

Russell Sadur, 31

Stephen Smith, 98

Stockbyte, 279

Tooga, 163, 215

Turqueti, 186

Tanya Zouev, 226

iStockphoto
Adisa, 261

Adventtr, 75

Carlos Alvarez, 165 (top)

Andyd, 165 (bottom)

Ansonsaw, 251

Atilayunal, 232

Adam36, 82

Billberryphotography, 253

Candu, 183

Jeffrey Coolidge, 172

Crazychristina, 244

Creativeye99, 33

Danveld, 158

Deepblue4you, 103

Devonyu, 167, 225

Robynmac, 196

Ryzhkov, 141

Sandoclr, 219

Debbi Smirnoff, 273

Spfoto, 262

Stock Shop Photography, 265

Tacojim, 191

Thepropshoppe, 199

Topdeq, 73

Vicm, 135

Viktar, 175

Webking, 38 (bottom)

Wragg, 231

Stockfood

Andrea Bricco, 88

Stephan Caraccio, 90

Crystal Cartier, 156

Cimba, 130

Sandra Eckhardt, 179

Eising Food Photography, 211

Foodcollection, 97, 137

Susanne Schanz, 229

Maximilian Stock, 81

Usbeck, 207

Shutterstock

Elkostas, 19

Fotomak 10 (top)

Kuppa, 14

Studio D

27 (bottom), 80, 120

Jesus Ayala, 87, 115

David Cook, 92

Chris Eckert, 117 (top), 145, 164 (top)

Philip Friedman, 12, 26, 29 (left), 37 (top), 38, 39, 45, 67, 83, 94, 129, 149, 213, 239

Charlotte Jenks Lewis, 28

Marko Metzinger, 25, 132 (top)

J Muckle, 91, 242

Lara Robby, 9, 20, 24, 27 (top), 29 (right), 35, 105, 132 (middle), 182

Kevin Sweeney, 15

Stuart Tyson, 113

Jeffrey Westbrook, 21, 38 (top), 117 (bottom)

Superstock

Fotosearch, 209

Dasha Wright

61

HEARST BOOKS
New York

An Imprint of Sterling Publishing
387 Park Avenue South
New York, NY 10016

Good Housekeeping

Rosemary Ellis	Editor in Chief
Richard Eisenberg	Special Projects Director
Sherry Akbar	Decorating Editor
The Good Housekeeping Research Institute	
John P. Kupsch, P.E.	Technical Director
Carolyn E. Forte	Home Appliances & Cleaning Products Director
Kathleen Huddy Sperduto	Textiles, Paper & Plastics Director

Book design by Matthew Papa

Library of Congress Cataloging-in-Publication Data
Soto, Anne Marie.
Good Housekeeping: stain removal : smart strategies
For getting rid of every stain every time/ Anne Marie Soto.
     p. cm.
Includes index.
1. Spotting (Cleaning) I. Good Housekeeping Institute (New York, N.Y.). II. Title.
TX324.S68 2006
648.1—dc22   2006011387

10 9 8 7 6 5 4 3 2 1

Good Housekeeping is a trademark of Hearst Communications, Inc.

www.goodhousekeeping.com

For information about custom editions, special sales, premium and corporate purchases, please contact Sterling Special Sales Department at 800-805-5489 or specialsales@sterlingpublishing.com.

Distributed in Canada by Sterling Publishing
c/o Canadian Manda Group, 165 Dufferin Street
Toronto, Ontario, Canada M6K 3H6

Distributed in Australia by Capricorn Link (Australia) Pty. Ltd.
P.O. Box 704, Windsor, NSW 2756 Australia

Manufactured in China

Sterling ISBN 978-1-58816-938-9

31901051192658